$700
BILLION
BAILOUT

$700 BILLION BAILOUT

The Emergency Economic Stabilization Act and
**What It Means to You,
Your Money, Your Mortgage,**
and **Your Taxes**

PAUL MUOLO

WILEY

John Wiley & Sons, Inc.

Published by John Wiley & Sons, Inc., Hoboken, New Jersey.
Published simultaneously in Canada.

For general information on our other products and services or for technical support, please contact our Customer Care Department within the United States at (800) 762-2974, outside the United States at (317) 572-3993 or fax (317) 572-4002.

Wiley also publishes its books in a variety of electronic formats. Some content that appears in print may not be available in electronic books. For more information about Wiley products, visit our web site at www.wiley.com.

ISBN 978-0-470-46256-0

Printed in the United States of America.

10 9 8 7 6 5 4 3 2 1

*For the American public and the few
who saw this disaster coming*

Contents

Author's Note   The $700 Billion Bailout Bill:
What Is This Monster?   ix

Introduction   Original Sin: The Emergency Economic
Stabilization Act of 2008: The Patriot
Act Meets the World of Finance   1

Chapter 1   **The Big Hoist: Will the $700 Billion Bailout
of the Mortgage and Credit Markets Work?
(It Had Better)**   **11**

   How the $700 Billion Bailout Machine Will Work
and Who Will Enforce It   14

   How TARP Will Work   16

   Will the Taxpayers Ever Get Their
$700 Billion Back?   24

   Should Fannie and Freddie Be Eliminated?   28

Chapter 2   **The Three Most Important Things You Need to
Know Now—Mortgages, Rates, and Housing**   **31**

   The Bailout Bill: First, the Good News   36

   Call Up Your Lender and Shout, "I Want to
Restructure My Mortgage!"   41

   The Bad News: Getting a Mortgage Is Going to
Be Much Tougher   46

   A Word about Interest Rates   48

Falling Home Values   50

The Wealthy Will Not Escape Unscathed   51

The Silver Lining: Falling Home Prices Mean

    Bargains for Some   52

How Will We Know When Home Prices Have

    Stopped Falling?   53

Chapter 3   **Where to Put Your Money Now**

(Hint: Not in a Vacation Home)   **55**

The Day the Flipping Stopped   58

The Contrarian Play in Vacation Homes   61

Investing in Foreclosures   62

Stocks: Is Now the Time to Get In?   63

Once You Decide to Jump In . . .   67

Safe Havens: Ginnie Mae and Treasury Bond

    Mutual Funds   68

A Word about Gold   70

The Safest Haven of All: CDs and Savings

    Accounts in Federally Insured Banks, S&Ls,

    and Credit Unions   70

Chapter 4   **Taxes and Politics: EESA Digs a Deeper**

Money Hole for All of Us   **73**

What Tax "Bennies" Were Actually Given Away?   76

What Do All These Tax Breaks Mean for

    the Consumer?   81

The Last Word: Politics   83

Epilogue   **The Last Word: If I Ran the Regulatory Zoo**   87

Excerpts from the Emergency Economic Stabilization
Act of 2008   **91**

Glossary of Terms and Agencies   **177**

About the Author   **187**

Author's Note

The $700 Billion Bailout Bill

What Is This Monster?

B y writing this book I get a second crack at the greatest financial disaster facing our nation since the Great Depression—the mortgage and credit crisis of 2008. As I consider my thoughts, stock markets have crashed worldwide, unemployment is rising, home prices continue to head south, and many Americans (unless they make their living off of home foreclosures) feel like there is no end in sight to the bad economic news. To many of us, it feels like we're on a ship that is taking on water. We're sinking, but there are repair crews in scuba gear trying to patch the holes in the bow. As passengers we're not sure if the ship can be saved.

In July 2008 Matthew Padilla of the *Orange County Register* and I produced a book called *Chain of Blame: How Wall Street Caused the Mortgage and Credit Crisis* (John Wiley & Sons). We made the radio and talk show circuit, got on *The Lou Dobbs Show*, *Fresh Air* with Terry Gross, Fox Business Network, and *The News Hour with Jim Lehrer*, among other programs. Our premise, laid out in *Chain of Blame*, is that Wall Street firms caused the greatest financial crisis any of us face because they needed to create more bonds to sell and turned to one of the largest debt markets in the world—home mortgages. Firms like Bear Stearns, Lehman Brothers, and Merrill Lynch picked the riskiest part of the mortgage market to securitize, subprime loans—mortgages given to people with bad credit. In Washington none of the regulators were paying much attention.

The Wall Street firms—and many of the lenders they bought home mortgages from—didn't care about the quality of the loans they were securitizing. That was our premise in *Chain of Blame*. We told the tale through the people at the center of the crisis: the executives and bond traders at Bear, Merrill, Lehman, and other Wall Street firms and at some of the lending firms. A few short months after our book was published, our premise was validated. Now, there's the aftermath to deal with: How do we fix this mess and prevent it from happening again?

On Friday, October 3, 2008, President Bush signed the Emergency Economic Stabilization Act (EESA), a 451-page bill whose original mission was to create a means for dealing with the problem. (We've conveniently reprinted part of the bill at the back of this book.) The bill's solution focuses on setting up a Troubled Asset Relief Program (TARP) inside the U.S. Treasury Department to buy delinquent mortgage assets (bonds as well as loans) from a variety of sellers, including both banks and Wall Street firms. It also allows the government (the Treasury, that is) to buy ownership stakes in banks to prop up their capital. Why do that? Treasury, led by former Wall Streeter Henry Paulson, believes those banks, armed with cash, will go out and make new loans to businesses and consumers and revive the economy. That's the great hope. The cost of this experiment to the taxpayers: $700 billion.

But the Emergency Economic Stabilization Act is more than a "let's buy mortgages and invest in banks" plan. It establishes a process for selling mortgages to the government in a way where supposedly the private sector will not unjustly profit by exploiting the legislation's loopholes. It also offers some hope for homeowners facing foreclosure by rewriting their mortgages. And there's more. The great secret of EESA is this: Most of the bill (300-plus pages out of 451) offers tax breaks to businesses and consumers that had nothing to do with the mortgage and credit crisis.

This book is about EESA—what it does, and what effect the current financial malaise will have on your home and your ability to get a mortgage going forward; on your savings, retirement plans, and investments; and on your taxes. The interesting thing about the bill is that its intended goal is to create a sense of financial stability in our financial markets, or maybe a façade of stability. Yet, it does nothing whatsoever to regulate or re-regulate our nation's financial institutions to prevent this from happening again. We face two nightmares: what this bill potentially allows, and what would happen if we as a nation do nothing at all.

PAUL MUOLO

$700 BILLION BAILOUT

Introduction

Original Sin: The Emergency Economic Stabilization Act of 2008

The Patriot Act Meets the World of Finance

The message on the woman's red T-shirt boiled down the issue to a political slogan: "Help for Main Street, Not Wall Street." Sitting in a government hearing room, she was a member of ACORN, an activist organization that for years had been staging protests outside bank branches in the streets of Washington and elsewhere, arguing that too many of the nation's mortgage lenders had been engaged in so-called predatory lending practices—that is, granting home mortgages to consumers who wouldn't be able to repay them. Over the past two years the group, whose initials stood for Association of Community Organizations for Reform Now, had a new cause—foreclosures.

Foreclosures were the by-product of all those predatory mortgages the group had warned about.*

Americans were losing their personal residences at a rate not seen since the Great Depression. Tent cities were beginning to spring up in cities like Las Vegas, once the hottest housing market in the country, one where homes that hadn't even finished construction were being flipped for 20 percent more than the contract price. But the economic boom was over.

The housing bust had become a national story, played out on the nightly news seven days a week. Unemployment was rising to multi-year highs. A few weeks earlier, gasoline had been selling for $4 a gallon in California. Even the nightly news shows, which hated doing financial stories because there was no good video to show the viewers, had finally latched onto the story. America's financial meltdown—with the housing and mortgage industry front and center—was suddenly sexy. It was also a political issue in a historic presidential election that pitted the first African-American candidate against a former war hero who had chosen a woman for his running mate. The entire country was now watching. So, too, was the rest of the world. And the Dow Jones Industrial Average was headed south like a cannon ball.

On the morning of September 23, 2008, the woman with the red T-shirt was not alone. She was accompanied by 20 other members of ACORN, some wearing T-shirts matching hers, others shouting out the slogans printed on their chests. (Yet others were there to protest the war in Iraq.) The setting wasn't a courthouse but rather the Dirksen Senate Office Building, a block from the U.S. Capitol, where all 21 members of the Senate Banking Committee had convened a hearing. It was 9:45.

---

*Even though ACORN was known more for its roots as a housing and mortgage activist, it found itself in the news during the presidential election of 2008 because of allegations that it had engaged in voter registration fraud. Election officials in a handful of states were looking into charges that ACORN workers submitted false registration forms for fictitious characters, including one Mickey Mouse. ACORN officials denied that it engaged any type of systematic fraud but admitted that some of its workers may have turned in duplicate or fake voter applications to pad their pay.

Sitting mostly in the hearing room's back rows, the ACORN protesters, left-leaning for sure, were beginning to get restless.

A block away at the Capitol building, tourists were already snapping pictures on a warm fall morning. But outside the hearing room 30 cameramen, several from foreign news bureaus, had parked their tripods and wide-angle lenses, waiting to hear not just the views of the 21 members of the Senate who made up the Banking Committee but also those of the two most powerful men in the world of finance: Treasury secretary Henry Paulson—the former head of Goldman Sachs—and Federal Reserve chairman Ben Bernanke, a former professor who once chaired the economics department at Princeton University. Two years earlier he had been picked by President George W. Bush to replace the legendary Alan Greenspan. ("Formerly legendary" might be a more appropriate description. Greenspan, known as the Maestro for his smooth shepherding of the economy, was now taking heat for not spotting the telltale signs of the housing bubble while he was in office.)

Along with Paulson and Bernanke, two other men would be testifying to the Senate that morning: Christopher Cox, chairman of the Securities and Exchange Commission, and James Lockhart, director of the Federal Housing Finance Agency, a Washington regulatory agency whose mission was to oversee Fannie Mae and Freddie Mac. Fannie and Freddie, as they were known, were two large government-chartered companies that bought mortgages from banks, savings and loans (S&Ls), nonbank mortgage lenders, and credit unions. By purchasing newly originated loans, they replenished the coffers of lenders, who could use that money to go out and make new loans. Fannie and Freddie, though, had effectively failed. On September 7 the government—Lockhart's agency with an assist from Treasury—had swooped in and taken control. Uncle Sam now owned them. Fannie and Freddie guaranteed (a synonym for "insured") or owned $5.4 trillion of the nation's $9.6 trillion in outstanding home mortgages, making them the linchpin of the U.S. mortgage market.

The 21 senators sitting on the committee wanted to know what the hell had happened. For the first time in what seemed like decades, all

21 senators on the committee were present for a hearing. Most times, 10 or so senators might show for a hearing, make a few statements for the C-SPAN cameras, and depart, leaving four or five colleagues (sometimes even fewer) to do what was called "the people's work."

Topic A that morning was the government seizure of Fannie and Freddie—a serious issue for sure. But Topic B was an even bigger issue of colossal proportion: Treasury secretary Paulson was now asking the nation's 535 elected officials for an emergency cash infusion of $700 billion to help stabilize Wall Street and the shaky banking industry. The crisis had emanated from the nation's housing mess, which had been caused by Wall Street backing too many subprime lenders just so they could create bonds from their loans. Wall Street firms like Bear Stearns, Lehman Brothers, and Merrill Lynch hadn't been careful enough about the loans they were buying that would go into those bonds. All three were now extinct or on the verge of being sold.

The public, as might be expected, was hopping mad. Spend $700 billion to bail out Wall Street? Not only did it make a good T-shirt slogan, but it fit on a bumper sticker as well. Treasury secretary Paulson needed the money so he could buy what he called "troubled" assets (mostly mortgage bonds) from hundreds of financial institutions. The way he described the situation to the public was that the capital markets—Wall Street and the nation's banks—had a major clogged artery. The patient (the economy), he reasoned, would have a heart attack if Treasury didn't have the resources (the $700 billion) to buy troubled mortgages from lenders. Paulson's plan was to give that money to the banks, which would use it to go out and make new loans—to businesses, to homeowners—to unclog that bad artery in the capital markets. He was also asking for permission for the government to buy ownership stakes in some banks. He hoped it wouldn't come to that, though.

To Senator Jim Bunning, a Republican from Kentucky, the whole idea sounded like a communist takeover of the U.S. banking system. "It's financial socialism and it's un-American," he told Paulson, his beet-red face turning darker.

But to hear Paulson tell it, he was trying to avoid a financial Armageddon. The former Goldman Sachs chief came across as someone who knew what he was talking about. After all, he had run Goldman Sachs for several years as the company earned billions. But Paulson had blemishes on his record. A year earlier he was serving as the White House's water boy on the then-emerging subprime crisis, making speeches in the United States and abroad, saying the nation's subprime mess was "contained"—that it wouldn't affect what he called the nation's "healthy economy." He had been dead wrong. And now he wanted $700 billion to help fix the problem.

But on this morning the senators weren't about to bring up Paulson's track record; a few of them had PR problems of their own. Committee chairman Christopher Dodd, a Democrat from Connecticut, had received a so-called Friend of Angelo (FOA) loan from Countrywide Financial Corporation, once the nation's largest subprime originator. Being a friend of Angelo Mozilo (the chairman and CEO) meant that Dodd received a price break on his own personal mortgage. Mozilo, silver-haired and a dapper dresser, was a 40-year veteran of mortgage lending. He was also now under investigation by the Feds for selling $400 million in company stock while Countrywide's fortunes tanked. (In July Countrywide was bought by Bank of America. If it hadn't been for the sale, Countrywide eventually would have filed for bankruptcy. Mozilo was now retired.)

The FOA story was receiving wide media attention. Dodd wasn't looking too good; neither was fellow senator Charles Schumer of New York, whose constituents on Wall Street had donated generously to his campaigns over the years. Schumer, ever a homer for the people of New York, had done nothing with his political power to rein in Wall Street. It was lucky for Schumer and Dodd that they weren't up for reelection this year. Neither would be too tough on Paulson.

As the hearing got under way, each senator had a chance to grandstand, making short speeches. The political theater was broadcast on C-SPAN for all the voters back home. Most of the senators were indignant about having to spend $700 billion of the public's money for something most Americans didn't understand. Dodd led off the hearing, calling Paulson's Troubled Asset Relief Program (TARP) "stunning for its lack of detail." The former Goldman Sachs chief had started his idea for the bailout legislation by typing out a brief three-page memo a couple of weeks earlier. Dodd wanted to know what Treasury would do if the bailout plan didn't work.

Senator Schumer, looking out for his constituents back home on Wall Street, pontificated that the "lowly mortgage" was at the center of what was not an international banking crisis. But he begrudgingly admitted, "The real danger is if we don't act." (Schumer loved grandstanding. It was often joked in Washington that the most dangerous place inside the Beltway was getting between Chuck Schumer and a camera.)

Meanwhile, the ACORN protestors in the hearing room were getting noisy. Every time a senator expressed the wish that the money be used to help the homeowners who were losing their houses, they'd shout an "Amen!" or a loud "Yes!" But Dodd, who was running the hearing, wasn't in a mood to hear their protests and the "Amen!" shouts. He banged his gavel. "You settle down or I'll clear this room," he warned.

The senators' opening speeches continued. Robert Menendez of New Jersey cautioned that he wouldn't be "stampeded into rubberstamping" Paulson's $700 billion TARP plan. Elizabeth Dole, a Republican from South Carolina, who was married to former presidential candidate (and Viagra pitchman) Bob Dole, tried to point the finger of blame on the crisis toward Fannie Mae and Freddie Mac, which many Democrats had gone to bat for over the years. She angrily recalled how she and her fellow Republicans had tried to push for stronger oversight of Fannie and Freddie. Dole, who was in a close reelection race that fall, was stretching the truth. Fannie and Freddie hadn't caused the subprime crisis, though the two had been unwise enough to buy $180 billion in subprime bonds.

By the time Paulson finally spoke, 90 minutes had passed. The protestors from ACORN had calmed down. Some had left the room. He thanked the senators for giving him what he called a "bazooka"— that is, the legislative authority—to take control of Fannie and Freddie. He implored them to move forward with the legislation for the $700 billion. "I'm convinced it will cost far less than the alternative," he said.

There was just one problem. The Senate didn't get to vote on the $700 billion first. That was the job of the House of Representatives. Less than a week later, on Monday, September 29, the House voted. Nancy Pelosi, the Speaker of the House, thought she had enough votes—but by the time the tally came up she was 23 short. The $700 billion bailout package was nixed 228 to 205. The revolt was led by proud conservatives from the Republican Party who said their offices had been inundated by telephone calls from angry citizens back home who didn't want their tax dollars used to bail out Wall Street. It was just like the ACORN T-shirts had said.

There was only one problem with the Republicans' defiance: They cast their votes while the stock market was still open. By noon that day the vote was complete and the Dow Jones Industrial Average went into a full-scale meltdown, plunging 778 points—a record for a one-day drop. Billions of dollars in shareholder wealth had been wiped out. Now constituents were calling their elected officials in Washington with a new complaint: Their 401(k)s and personal investments had been hammered.

The tables had turned. Republicans were now under fire for *not* passing it. The Senate decided to take up the vote on Wednesday. By the time it did, the $700 billion legislation had changed: The version the House had turned down had been a streamlined bill (just over 110 pages) that dealt mostly with giving the Treasury secretary the power to buy troubled mortgages. This time around it was loaded down with pork-barrel legislation; quite a bit of it was tied to extending tax breaks for alternative energy and green fuels, but it also threw in a few benefits that Republicans might like, including tax breaks for the construction of race tracks (a nod to NASCAR dads) and for the coal industry.

On Wednesday the Senate approved the bill—which had ballooned to 451 pages—by a wide margin. Two days later the House voted, and it too passed the bill by a wide margin. Two hours later President Bush signed the bill. The Emergency Economic Stabilization Act (EESA) was now law. The United States was about to spend $700 billion to buy troubled mortgage assets. To get the bill passed quickly, Secretary Paulson had promised he could get most of the $700 billion back by holding those troubled assets for a few years and then selling them later at a profit or at least breaking even. But as Senator Dodd had pointed out, the bill was short on details. Even though Bush signed the bill, the stock market continued to suffer: It went down, down, down, experiencing losses not seen since the Great Depression.

■ ■ ■

Not since Congress had passed the Patriot Act in the wake of the 9/11 terrorist attacks had a piece of legislation moved so quickly with so little debate. And at $700 billion (unless Paulson was right and Treasury recouped that money over time), it would be the largest bailout in U.S. history—of any industry. The S&L crisis, which had occurred 20 years earlier, had cost a mere $120 billion.

But the new bill was about more than money. It was about power. In the name of national security, the Patriot Act gave law enforcement officials—for better or worse—more tools to spy on Americans and foreigners. Tom Myers, a forensic accountant who had worked on S&L fraud cases two decades earlier, drew an analogy between EESA and the Patriot Act. "It gives the government unfettered power," he said. But what was Myers talking about?

Not only does the bill give the government—the Treasury Department, which is running the program—$700 billion, but the bill also gives it the power to bail out counties and cities as long as these areas may have suffered increased "costs or losses in the current market turmoil." EESA's language also says Treasury can come to the aid of retirement funds. Well, what does that mean? Who really knows? EESA was written and passed so quickly that it is open to more interpretations than the Bible. The way it was pitched originally by Paulson, it was supposed to help only banks and Wall Street.

But one thing seems certain: For American taxpayers, the ability to obtain a mortgage has been severely damaged, as has the value of the real estate they own. The correction in the housing market could last up to 10 years. With the government takeover of Fannie and Freddie, the U.S. mortgage market has been socialized. It is under the control of the Treasury, which is controlled by the White House. All of this happened under the watch of a president who rode into office believing that deregulation and getting government off the backs of businesses was a laudable goal because companies could make good money and pass on the largesse to all citizens. It was part of what Bush had called "the ownership society." It looked good on paper. Now, the government owns the mortgage industry, more or less. That's called irony.

For a week and a half after Paulson got his money wish, the stock market kept declining in large chunks except for an occasional rebound. The Treasury secretary wasn't happy. The stock market kept on tanking. Paulson was hoping for a respite from the Dow's carnage. Some banks had stopped lending to each other and their business customers, exacerbating what was referred to as a credit crisis. On Tuesday morning, October 14, Paulson took one more bold step: He unveiled a plan to spend $250 billion of the money that was supposed to be used for buying troubled mortgages to instead invest in nine of the largest banks in the United States, including his former firm Goldman Sachs as well as Bank of America, Citigroup, Wells Fargo, and JPMorgan Chase. But few of these banks were in danger of failing. Paulson, according to the press reports of the day, strong-armed the heads of these banks, telling them it was their "patriotic duty" to go along with the idea. Treasury wasn't taking over these banks—but it was becoming a stakeholder. Paulson wanted to send a signal to the investment community and the world at large that the U.S. government was standing behind its banks. After these nine investments, hundreds more might follow.

To the men and the women on the street watching the news unfold, it all seemed surreal—nine of the nation's biggest and most respected banks had been partially nationalized. What did it all mean? Republicans weren't supposed to nationalize businesses. Hugo Chávez, the socialist leader of Venezuela, did stuff like that. Paulson had already spent more than one-third of the money that was supposed to buy troubled mortgages, money that could trickle down to the struggling homeowner. Of course, in late 2008 curing the nation's credit and mortgage crisis was no longer a worry for Paulson. With the election of Barack Obama as president, Paulson, a Republican and a Bush appointee, was out of a job. The cleanup—without a doubt—is the most important task facing the new Treasury secretary.

What follows in this book is a discussion of what the bailout means for your financial life. We've reprinted part of the bailout bill at the end of this book. Most of the news isn't good. As for the $700 billion being spent on your behalf, if Mr. Paulson's track record is any indication—especially his comments made in the summer of 2007 about the country's subprime crisis being "contained" and not spreading overseas—we, as a nation, are in serious trouble. It's now up to a new White House to serve as shepherd of the TARP program—an unproven creation for sure.

Chapter 1

The Big Hoist: Will the $700 Billion Bailout of the Mortgage and Credit Markets Work?

(It Had Better)

"It will work."
—Treasury secretary Henry Paulson, commenting after passage of
the $700 billion Emergency Economic Stabilization Act

"It should help."
—Überinvestor Warren Buffett, chairman of Berkshire Hathaway

On a Thursday morning in mid-March of 2008, Treasury secretary Henry Paulson called a press conference in Washington to discuss the results of a study done by the President's Working Group on Financial Markets, which consisted of his agency and three others: the Federal Reserve, the Securities and Exchange Commission (SEC), and the Commodity Futures Trading Commission

(CFTC).* Seven months earlier, Paulson had been pushing the Bush administration's line that the country's subprime mortgage crisis would not spill over to other parts of the economy or world economies. But on this morning, finally, the former Goldman Sachs CEO came clean. The setting: the National Press Club Building in downtown Washington, two blocks east of the White House on F Street, a block away from the Treasury building. Reporters from every major news organization in the United States and several overseas news outlets were there.

The report he was discussing that morning before 50 reporters and TV cameramen (who were broadcasting live) had concluded: "The turmoil in financial markets clearly was triggered by a dramatic weakening of underwriting standards for U.S. subprime mortgages, beginning in late 2004 and extending into early 2007." The report's diagnosis singled out the credit rating agencies (Fitch Ratings Ltd., Standard & Poor's, and Moody's Investors Service) and "those involved" in securitizing subprime. The diagnosis bullet-point section of the report never once used the phrases *Wall Street* or *investment bankers*. As the former head of Goldman Sachs, Paulson wasn't about to gut the beast that he once worked for. He still had good friends there.

The Treasury secretary told the press that securitization had paved the way for lower-cost mortgages to be made to millions of Americans, but also complained about what he called "extreme complexity" of financial instruments—credit default swaps (CDSs), among other instruments—and a lack of transparency for investors. A credit default swap is an insurance contract that allows an investor to bet or hedge against losses. There were $44 trillion worth (that's not a typo) of these

---

*The SEC regulates financial disclosures by publicly traded lenders but not necessarily their businesses. The CFTC regulates commodities markets, including the trading of instruments that represent commodities. The Federal Reserve is the nation's central bank, whose job it is to set monetary policy and fight inflation. It also regulates banks.

contracts outstanding in the United States at last count. By comparison, the U.S. government, which is deeply in debt, owes just over $10.2 trillion on the outstanding Treasury bonds sold to finance the nation's debt. The government funds the country's operations, including paying for its defense and cutting all those Social Security checks each month.

Credit default swaps can be written by just about anyone, but usually it's insurance firms or investment banking houses. American International Group (AIG), the large insurance conglomerate (which is now owned by us, the taxpayers), wrote plenty of CDS insurance policies. When AIG—a company with $1 trillion in assets—was taken over by the government (a deal Paulson also helped put together) it had (outstanding) $70 billion in contracts or bets on subprime bonds. Would AIG be able to cover all those bets if the subprime bonds it insured went south? That's a good question, but here's an even more important question: Who regulates the CDS market? The SEC? The CFTC? Answer: *Not one government agency keeps tabs on this market,* which is why no one ever thought to look at AIG—whose primary business is insurance (including annuities to retirees)—to see if it had enough capital to cover its swap policies. (Unbeknownst to most consumers, AIG also owns two subprime lending companies, both of which are not the property of Uncle Sam.)

At the National Press Club, the Treasury secretary also blamed investors for not knowing what they were buying and cautioned that whatever regulatory changes might lie ahead, the Treasury, under his direction, would not stifle "financial innovation" in the marketplace, which meant that the creation of and trading in such instruments as credit default swaps (used to hedge or speculate, depending on what the customer wanted to do) would continue.

The next day Bear Stearns' stock plunged, and within days the government had arranged its sale to JPMorgan Chase. Six months later, President Bush signed the EESA legislation, committing the $700 billion. Ben Bernanke's team at the Federal Reserve had put together the Bear sale, consulting with Paulson over at Treasury. Paulson's former employer, Wall Street giant Goldman Sachs, had smartly avoided getting too heavily involved in financing nonbank subprime lenders and securitizing their mortgages into bonds—also known as mortgage-backed securities (MBSs) or asset-backed securities (ABSs).* But Goldman had been a bottom-fisher in this debacle, buying—for an undisclosed amount—a specialty servicer called Litton Loan Servicing. Based in Houston, Texas, Litton was the brainchild of an industry veteran named Larry Litton, whose son now ran the firm. The company's forte was servicing subprime loans for companies that were stuck with bad mortgages, especially delinquent subprime mortgages. It was a fee-based business. Banks love fee-based businesses.

KEY ISSUE

As for investors not knowing what they were buying—Paulson's words—the Treasury Department under the Emergency Economic Stabilization Act (EESA) would begin buying the very same assets. But will the U.S. Treasury Department have a handle on the troubled assets to which it is committing taxpayer money? Will it know what it is buying? And will the government not overpay for mortgages? Only time will tell.

How the $700 Billion Bailout Machine Will Work and Who Will Enforce It

The last thing in the world Republicans like to do is create permanent government jobs. It drives them crazy. It's part of who they are. Never mind that after 9/11 President Bush and a willing Congress restructured

---

*A mortgage-backed security (MBS) usually refers to a mortgage bond that is backed by A paper or good credit quality loans. Asset-backed security (ABS) is reserved for subprime mortgages or other receivables.

our federal law enforcement troops, creating the Department of Homeland Security, now one of the largest employers in all of government with 183,000 workers. Full-time government jobs paying benefits and retirement just means more government costs. Republicans hate stuff like that. As I've already noted, the great irony of this crisis is that the back end of the U.S. mortgage market—the companies (Fannie Mae and Freddie Mac) that buy home mortgages from lenders that deal with the public—is now in the hands of the government. The system has been socialized. The $700 billion effort to buy ailing mortgage assets from banks, investment banks, S&Ls, and other financial institutions is called the Troubled Asset Relief Program (TARP).

But, there is more to it than that. Even though the idea is to help ailing banks, the bill is so generally written it appears the Treasury has the authority to buy troubled assets (and not only mortgages) from:

- Counties
- Cities
- Retirement plans
- Foreign banks
- Foreign governments

These last two have not received much play in the media.

And as already covered, Uncle Sam has bought ownership stakes in banks—preferred stock. President Bush's chief economic adviser, Edward Lazear, promised that Uncle Sam would stay away from purchasing voting common stock and taking any seats on a bank's board of directors. (Directors are supposed to advise management on what types of loans they should be making.)

Henry Paulson and two of his top deputies at Treasury—Robert Steel and Neel Kashkari—in early 2008 actually began drawing up plans to create a Troubled Asset Relief Program (TARP) modeled after the Resolution Trust Corporation (RTC), the S&L bailout agency that sold $400 billion worth of assets (mostly commercial real estate and junk bonds) from 1989 to 1994. But Paulson never dreamed he'd ever have to actually use the plan. It was a contingency only. The EESA bill that President Bush signed does not create a new government agency. The TARP program created under EESA will be run out of the Treasury Department, which is a stone's throw from the White House. Its first director is Kashkari, a two-year veteran of Treasury who, like Paulson and Steel, used to work at Goldman Sachs. Before getting the job of running TARP, Kashkari was an assistant secretary of international affairs at Treasury. (At Goldman he did mergers and acquisitions work.) Assistant secretaries are appointed by the president and need Senate confirmation, and the same holds true of the TARP director, in this case Kashkari.

How TARP Will Work

So, the key questions are:

Will the government overpay for troubled mortgage assets so it can help certain banks?

Answer: The strategy is to buy mortgages, MBSs, and ABSs at a fair price. The government is paying cash here. The idea is that the bank selling its troubled mortgages, bonds, or whatever to the government will take that cash and go out and make new loans, whether they are loans to a commercial business like a steel mill or an auto dealership, or more mortgages. This, in theory, will alleviate the credit crunch. The government can buy troubled assets (securities, whole loans, etc.) direct or it can hold what's called a reverse auction where many different banks might bring their similar troubled mortgages to Treasury at the same time. Treasury can evaluate all the assets and offer the lowest price it can. If the selling bank doesn't like the price Treasury is offering, it won't have to sell. However, if Treasury is really serious about helping these banks get back on their feet by taking bad assets off their hands, it probably won't be too tough on price. It has to balance overpaying (to help banks) with being prudent about using the taxpayers' money. Many eyes will be watching.

I'm not sure I understand this. The Treasury is using $700 billion of taxpayer money to buy troubled mortgage assets from banks and Wall Street firms. Where did all these troubled assets come from? What's wrong with them that only the government will now buy them?

Answer: Many of these troubled assets—at least the ones that have been talked about publicly—are bonds backed by subprime mortgages. Some are nonconforming mortgages (non-A paper credit quality) such as payment option ARMs (POAs), stated-income loans, and alt-A mortgages. They were packaged into bonds mostly by Wall Street firms that then sold them to investors. But many Street firms also kept them as an investment for their own balance sheets—or were forced to do so because they could no longer find buyers for these bonds. In the case of subprime, a large percentage of the mortgages that went into these bonds are now delinquent. The nationwide delinquency rate on subprime mortgages is above of 30 percent. Because the loans are delinquent, the cash flow coming off these bonds falls way short of what the investors in these bonds had anticipated. This has caused the value of these bonds to fall—so much so that the banks holding them are forced to mark them down in value (this practice is called mark-to-market accounting) and take losses on them. Because they have fallen in value by so much, in most cases no one will buy them from the firms holding them (investment banks like Merrill Lynch and Morgan Stanley). In some cases there have been potential buyers for these bonds, but the price offered might be so low (20 cents on the dollar) that the banks holding these assets refuse to sell at such a large loss; they think, at worst, these troubled mortgage assets might be worth (for example) 60 cents on the dollar.

Does the government think these bonds will come back in value?

Answer: The Treasury Department is not expected to buy troubled mortgage bonds at 100 cents on the dollar. It has said that publicly. Contractors working for the government will review the troubled loans backing (collateralizing) these bonds and come up with a fair price for the seller. If Treasury thinks a bond is worth only 70 cents on the dollar, it might offer 65 cents to the seller. The government will then hope to sell it for 5 cents more (at 70 cents on the dollar) in a year or so or when prices improve.

Wasn't there insurance on these bonds that Wall Street created?

Answer: Yes. But the bond insurance companies that wrote the policies—firms like Ambac, Financial Guaranty Insurance Company (FGIC), and MBIA Inc.—are now in trouble financially and cannot pay off on all the insurance policies they wrote. (These firms never anticipated that the underlying subprime mortgages would have delinquency rates above 10 percent, much less 30 percent. They also had no history of writing these policies and in most cases got into this business only five years ago.)

What is a credit crunch? The media keep using that phrase to describe this crisis.

Answer: A credit crunch is a situation where businesses (in particular, companies with good prospects of turning a profit) cannot get loans easily or at reasonable rates. The same lack of money to lend can apply to consumers as well. Some banks are making it harder for their customers to obtain credit cards, for instance. Banks have been hoarding cash instead of lending it out. That's what the Treasury Department wants to avoid. The government figures lending out money to businesses will spur economic growth. When the economy regains strength, businesses will hire more workers, and those employees, in turn, will go out and buy things—like houses. That's that the theory, at least. The whole TARP plan rests on that premise, a theory.

Will Treasury use its own employees to buy mortgage assets from Wall Street, banks, and other sellers?

Answer: No. Ex-Goldman vice president Kashkari is the first director of the Troubled Asset Relief Program. He's the boss who has to sign off on asset purchases, but the Treasury does not employ any full-time mortgage traders who buy and sell assets. Until this crisis, Treasury was not in the business of purchasing and selling assets from U.S. banks and Wall Street firms. For years we've been told that the smartest mortgage traders (men and women who buy and sell mortgage bonds and pools of whole loans) work on Wall Street. This includes the big boys such at Bear Stearns (almost failed, but now part of JPMorgan Chase), Lehman Brothers (now in bankruptcy), Merrill Lynch (now part of Bank of America). Then there are the smaller boutique firms like BlackRock Inc. and PIMCO, which aren't exactly household names. These firms are the ones that will be the market makers, the companies buying and selling subprime bonds and mortgage assets on behalf of the government.

AN UGLY FACT

One of the first outside contractors the Treasury hired to help it manage the auctions is Bank of New York Mellon, which is one of the nine megabanks it partly nationalized in mid-October. In other words, Treasury gave a government contract to a bank that it owns part of. To some lawyers that might look like a conflict of interest, but EESA—with its Patriot Act–like fail-safes—allows for waivers from what's called the Federal Acquisition Regulation (FAR). Translation: The government can do what it wants.

Will there be any watchdog group overseeing the bailout effort to make sure the government (the Treasury Department) doesn't screw up?

Answer: The bailout bill mandates that Congress must create an oversight panel to keep an eye on TARP's operations. The five-member panel will include overseers appointed by the Speaker and the minority leader of the House, the Senate majority and minority leaders, and one person picked by both the Speaker and the majority leader of the Senate. The bill offers no guidance on what type of people might be appointed to the panel and no prohibitions on political cronyism. If they want, the board can hire outside consultants. There is a cap—based on what is called "Level 1 of the Executive Schedule"—on how much pay the board members can receive annually. That works out to $186,000 a year apiece. Among its powers the oversight panel can:

- Commission staff from other government agencies to work for it.
- Hold hearings on the Treasury's TARP effort and request information.
- Issue reports based on its findings.

The panel will shut down its operations six months after the bailout is completed. The five members are entitled to government expense accounts, too. Even members of Congress can serve on the oversight board, but they cannot receive extra pay for their time.

As an aside, the Treasury has the power to form an office of inspector general inside the agency to keep an eye on how Kashkari and his successors, if any, manage the purchase and sale of mortgages under TARP. The inspector general must be appointed by the president of the United States.

The inspector general's office must:

- Keep a list of which banks, financial institutions, and others the government buys mortgages from.

- Explain why Treasury deemed it necessary to purchase troubled assets from each seller.
- Provide what's called "detailed biographical information" on each asset manager Treasury hires. (This last requirement could be interesting.)

I heard somewhere that the government can spend more than $700 billion. Is that true?

Answer: Even though the government has the authority to use up to $700 billion in taxpayer money to buy troubled mortgage assets from lenders, it actually has the ability to spend more—billions more—but not at once. This is how it could work: Let's say a year from now the Treasury's TARP program is tapped out and has spent the entire $700 billion, including the $250 billion to partially nationalize some U.S. banks. It can actually sell some of the assets it bought, raise money on those sales, and replenish its bailout fund. If it sells $5 billion in subprime bonds it bought from Merrill Lynch to a private investor and clears $5.2 billion on the sale, it now can use that fresh money to go out and buy more subprime bonds, ailing mortgages, and auto loans—whatever it needs.

This replenishment process can be perpetuated for several years as long as Treasury doesn't exceed—at any one time—the $700 billion figure mandated by the EESA law. The legislation signed by President Bush states that the authority (the money) "shall be limited to $700,000,000,000 outstanding at any one time." I'm not sure most members of Congress and senators who voted for the bill (or even President Bush) realized what this means. Representative Barney Frank, the Democrat from Massachusetts who chairs the House committee that oversees banking, once made this fact public in a television interview after the bill passed, but I'm not sure it has sunk in. (Rep. Frank is what's called a policy wonk, someone who actually reads and understands legislation. In years past he was also a big supporter of Fannie Mae and Freddie Mac, so he has his flaws.)

So, why do we need to invest $125 billion in our largest banks, even though most of them have enough capital?

Answer: On Monday, October 13, the chief executives of the nine largest banks and investment banking houses in the country walked into a conference room at the Treasury Department and were handed a one-page document that said they agreed to sell shares in their companies to Uncle Sam. Several of these bankers, who talked to the press without their names being disclosed, said they were floored. Paulson told them they had to sign it before they left the building that afternoon. They all complied, some begrudgingly. The next day when Paulson announced the plan to the world he said, "We regret having to take these actions."

Roughly $125 billion would be used to invest in the nine banks. Another $125 billion would be used to invest in other banks and S&Ls, presumably only institutions that had a chance of surviving the crisis. Credit unions, those nonprofit lenders that are technically owned by their members, aren't even mentioned in the bill.

If the U.S. government is buying troubled mortgage assets, why do we need to also put money into these nine banks, especially if some don't want or need the money?

Answer: There are a few ways to get the economy moving again—that is, to get banks to lend money to businesses. One way is to get someone powerful in government—the president of the United States or, say, the Treasury secretary—to jawbone the markets. A leader with credibility can call up the bankers across the country and tell them to start lending again. This is called jawboning. Sometimes such a move might work. It would appear that Paulson doesn't have that kind of juice in the banking industry. That's why he needed the EESA bill and the TARP program. The U.S. Treasury cannot move markets by just talking. Paulson has tried this in the past and it has failed. He blew his

Just because the government is buying stakes in nine banks—Bank of America, Citigroup, JPMorgan Chase, and Wells Fargo being among the largest—that doesn't mean these banks have to use that money to make new loans. The Treasury secretary is praying that they do.

capital with investors when he predicted that the country's subprime crisis would not spread overseas.

Why didn't Paulson mention this bank nationalization plan earlier when he was talking about the Treasury Department buying troubled assets from banks? Is that supposed to free up capital, too?

Answer: Republicans do not like the idea of the government owning stakes in private-sector financial institutions. It goes against their basic core belief in free markets. Federal Reserve chairman Ben Bernanke, early on, was in favor of the Treasury Department owning stakes in banks, but Paulson resisted. As the stock market continued to spiral downward in October, Bernanke convinced Paulson on one key point: that lending is about leverage. An amount of cash can go a long way. If Treasury, for instance, makes a $10 billion investment in a bank, that gives the bank leverage because that bank can now go out and lend $100 billion on that $10 billion. It's similar to a consumer having a 10 percent down payment and borrowing 90 percent on a home purchase. Why this didn't dawn on Paulson earlier is unclear.

If the government invests in a bank by purchasing preferred stock, what prevents that bank from using the money to buy

other banks instead of lending it out to businesses to spur the economy?

Answer: Nothing. That is one of the sad realities of the $700 billion Troubled Asset Relief Program. There are no strings attached to the money these banks—Bank of America, Citigroup, Wells Fargo, and others—receive. They can even hoard the cash, a move that will not spur new lending to businesses and consumers.

Do we have any idea how many troubled mortgages (the dollar amount) the government (the Treasury Department) will wind up buying under this bailout?

Answer: We do not. When the Treasury secretary first pitched the "we'll buy troubled mortgages" idea to Congress, the thought was that banks would take the cash they received for those troubled assets and go out and make new loans, again to businesses and consumers. However, the plan has been changing constantly since it became law, which might lead some to question whether anyone in government has a clear vision of how to fix the mess. There is even talk about the government writing insurance policies to cover losses on delinquent mortgages that have been modified to help the homeowner. Under a modified loan, the interest rate and/or principal owed could be reduced, making the monthly payments lower for the consumer. Presumably, some of the $700 billion TARP money might go toward this effort.

Will the Taxpayers Ever Get Their $700 Billion Back?

If you watched the unraveling of the credit and mortgage crisis—and the ensuing stock market collapse—you may recall that when Henry Paulson first proposed the bailout plan he promised one thing: that the government *should* be able to get most of that money back for the taxpayer, all $700 billion worth.

The plan is supposed to work like this: Bank of America, which owns one of the biggest junk heaps of the mortgage crisis—that would be Angelo Mozilo's Countrywide Home Loans, which it bought back in July 2008 just before it headed for an almost certain bankruptcy—goes to Treasury and unloads $10 billion worth of delinquent payment option ARMs (POAs), the "I'll cry tomorrow" loans where consumers keep their monthly payments low by adding onto their total debt. Treasury pays 70 cents on the dollar ($7 billion), because its outside contractor analyzing the loans for the government (an investment banking firm, perhaps a boutique firm like BlackRock Inc.) thinks that in time housing values might flatten out and the loans aren't all that delinquent, so maybe that's a fair price. (The contractor will make its assessment based on huge databases that track home prices in every single zip code in the United States.)

If housing values do flatten out or even rise and the payment option ARMs that Treasury bought from Mozilo's old institution do not go sour in greater numbers, then that 70-cent price could hold water. Two years down the road Treasury sells the old Countrywide portfolio (which it bought from Bank of America, Countrywide's new owner) to, say, a large bank like Wells Fargo for the same 70 cents. The government breaks even—except when you factor in what it pays its asset manager, BlackRock. Any sale price under 70 cents on the dollar on the Countrywide portfolio results in a loss for the government; anything over, a gain. But it's all academic whether it's going to play out that way.

No one—including the Paulson, the Treasury Department, and any of its asset manager contractors in the private sector—have any idea where home prices will be six months or a year from now (take your pick). Their hope is to make money for the taxpayer. Their profits will rest on two things: what price they pay, and whether the mortgages or bonds purchased do not get any worse in terms of delinquencies.

Right now, a bank like Bank of America cannot unload its crummy mortgages to another bank in the private sector, because no bank will pay a fair price for those assets.

So the logical follow-up question is: Will speculators be able to buy troubled assets from ailing banks and flip them at a higher price to the government?

According to details of the bill, investors who want to sell assets to the Treasury Department cannot do so at a price higher than what they paid for them. In other words, an investor who buys discounted MBSs from a seller cannot turn around and then unload the bonds to Treasury at a higher price. However, the legislation leaves a loophole: If a seller of bad assets took control of mortgage bonds through a merger/acquisition or bought them out of a conservatorship, they are exempt from the Treasury's "unjust enrichment" clause. This means Bank of America, potentially, can flip assets to Treasury because when it bought Countrywide it did so by discounting the ailing mortgages that Countrywide held.

Lewis Ranieri, the well-respected former head of Salomon Brothers who helped invent the A paper mortgage-backed security (the one that's not likely to default), once opined that "mortgages are about math." So let's talk about the arithmetic of the crisis. There is roughly $1 trillion worth of outstanding subprime loans in the United States. Let's say half of them go bad, causing $500 billion in losses. There is roughly $400 billion worth of alt-A mortgages, which are like subprime mortgages but the borrower had a higher credit score. These aren't quite as risky as subprime mortgages, so let's say 25 percent or $100 billion worth of these go south. And there are home equity loans, which are going delinquent at a rapid rate, too. There's about $800 billion worth of those, and maybe $200 billion wind up worthless. Then there are the good credit quality A paper loans that are suffering, too. That could be another $100 billion, which brings us to $900 billion in losses. Let's add in another $100 billion just to be conservative. We're at $1 trillion in losses. To date, institutions (banks, Wall Street) have taken $500 billion in losses.

We're halfway there. But we haven't added in, yet, all those credit default swaps—those insurance contracts that were written to cover losses on mortgage bonds. Insurers like AIG have to pay off on those claims only if the underlying mortgages go bad, but we don't know how many really will go bad. We know only that there are $44 trillion worth of credit default swap contracts in the United States. But we don't know how many of those are on mortgages. There can be several bets against the same bond, extrapolating those losses out exponentially. Why don't we know the losses on credit default swap contracts on sub-prime loans? Answer: because not one government agency is in charge of the swaps market. You might say that this is the Death Star or black hole of our financial system. There is one thought that could make all those swaps nil: Treasury could order the contracts null and void. This would stop the huge payouts on these bets—but it will not stop home mortgages from going bust. The consumer is still on the hook.

But will we get the $700 billion back like Paulson said? Then again, the TARP program involves more than just buying troubled loans and bonds. If Treasury is spending at least $250 billion of taxpayer money to buy preferred stock in banks, S&Ls, Wall Street firms, insurance companies (and others potentially), it stands to reason it will get that investment back—at least that is the plan as explained by the Treasury secretary to the public. At the very least, the preferred stock Treasury holds in these firms pays a 5 percent dividend. That's money in the bank for taxpayers. Let's just hope that none of the banks the government "owns" a piece of goes south.

Pick the very first day the government buys a batch of mortgage assets. (By law, the sale price of assets bought by the government must be posted on the Treasury Department's web site within two days.) Mark that point in time. Pick the very last day the government sells its last troubled asset. Calculate the average home price drop between those two points in time. If the government program is run properly and home values decline 20 percent going forward, taxpayers will lose $140 billion of the $700 billion. It's all about home values. Homes are the collateral for mortgages.

Should Fannie and Freddie Be Eliminated?

Up until this financial crisis came to a head in the summer of 2008, most Americans probably couldn't even tell you what Fannie Mae and Freddie Mac were, much less what they do. When they were taken over by the Treasury Department and the Federal Housing Finance Agency (their regulator) on September 7, they become front page news, not to mention the butt of jokes on *Saturday Night Live, The Daily Show with Jon Stewart*, and numerous other comedy programs. In short, they had arrived—and they were close to being broke because they owned between them $180 billion in mortgage bonds backed by subprime loans.

Fannie and Freddie are two odd financial animals in the sense they have government charters but also are publicly traded stockholder-owned companies. They were created by Congress (with the permission of the president) many decades back to provide liquidity to the mortgage market. Because they were created by Congress, they often are referred to as government-sponsored enterprises (GSEs). They purchase home mortgages from savings and loans, banks, nondepository mortgage companies, credit unions, and the like. Once these lenders sell their loans to Fannie and Freddie, they receive cash and can use that money to go out and make more mortgage loans.

The thing is, if Fannie and Freddie didn't exist, lenders would be forced to keep mortgages on their books or securitize them through Wall Street or some other source. If a bank holds loans on its balance sheet, they must be offset with a liability—a funding source like a deposit account. Banks gather deposits from consumers and businesses and then lend that money out. It's just like in that Christmastime movie, *It's a Wonderful Life*. Without deposits, there would be no source of funds to make loans, at least at the banks and S&Ls. That's how banking works. The difference between a bank's cost of deposits and what it makes on a loan is its gross profit.

The reason the government bailed out Fannie and Freddie is their size. They hold $1.4 trillion in home mortgages or bonds on their books and they guarantee (put their insurance or backing) on another $4.2 trillion of home mortgages. Their cost of funds is debt—bonds that they've sold to investors. Fannie and Freddie do not take deposits from the public. They are needed in the housing finance system because given the current mess we're in, there is no one else of their size to absorb or perform their function.

But what do we do with them? The first thing to be done is to officially nationalize them. Prior to their takeover by the government there was only an *implicit* guarantee backing the two, which meant Uncle Sam, as a technical matter, did not have to make good on any of their obligations (their borrowings in the capital markets) if they went belly-up. They had government charters but were not government institutions supported by taxpayers. Even though the guarantee was perceived, it was not etched into law. Still, everyone on Wall Street believed if they went belly-up Uncle Sam would make good on at least some of their financial obligations, which is exactly what happened.

Various ideas have been floated by academics and politicians to either merge them into one or eventually fix them and sell them to the private sector. Given the depth of the financial crisis, the best immediate plan might entail breaking them up into four regional federal housing finance agencies that continue to buy mortgages from lenders. They would be tightly regulated and have caps on what they could pay their executives. They, more or less, would be run like public utilities and their profits (if I had my way) would be used to pay down the deficit each year.

KEY ISSUE

Even though Fannie and Freddie are now wards of the government, their regulator, the Federal Housing Finance Agency, is running them through what's called a conservatorship, which means they cannot spit without talking to their regulator. Their common stock still trades on the New York Stock Exchange, for around a $1 per share. Do not buy the shares thinking someday they will come back. They will not.

Chapter 2

The Three Most Important Things You Need to Know Now—Mortgages, Rates, and Housing

"In this house that I call home ..."
—John Doe of X (The Band)

The next time someone talks to you about the "American dream of home ownership," you may be tempted to slap that person in the face. That's the way it feels in the United States right now. The financial markets of the world's most powerful economies have been brought to their knees by the lowly home mortgage, a product that arrived on these shores back in 1831 by the way of England.*

---

*The first institution to actually make a mortgage was the Oxford Provident Building Association of Frankford, Pennsylvania, which was formed in 1831. The town of Frankford is now part of Philadelphia. American building associations (the forerunner of the savings and loan or building and loan) were tailored after building societies. In the 1920s there were 12,000 savings and loans. Today there are 900.

Under the guise of the $700 billion bailout bill, the U.S. government is now partly nationalizing some of the largest banks in the land—Bank of America, Citigroup, JPMorgan Chase, Bank of New York Mellon, Wells Fargo—even if they don't want the government's money. In mid-October when the nationalization plan was unveiled, Edward Lazear, chairman of the president's Council of Economic Advisers, stood on the White House lawn talking to reporters. Roughly $125 billion would be used to buy stakes in nine of the nation's largest banks, some of which are mentioned above. Another $125 billion would be spent to buy stakes in small and midsize banks and savings and loans (S&Ls). Yes, the government still plans on buying troubled mortgage assets from financial institutions—but now it would have $250 billion less to spend for that purpose. Lazear didn't rule out using the government's newfound money to purchase other bad loans, either, like auto and credit card loans. Welcome to the new capitalism.

Blame the King. Blame the dying king—Wall Street—for securitizing all those subprime loans without actually looking at the quality of mortgages the Wall Street firms were buying from the nation's lenders. Wall Street's rationalizations are streaming in, and they go like this: "We bought all those no-down-payment and stated-income loans made to people with questionable credit because we thought home prices would keep rising 20 percent a year." (With a stated-income loan, also called a liar loan, borrowers state their income and the mortgage companies, some of which were actually owned by Wall Street, believe them.)

Two centuries ago the goal was simple: allow people to purchase homes by putting a modest amount of money down—say 10 percent—and stretch out their payments over many years by cutting a check each month to a lender. This was called leverage. Put a little down and borrow a lot. Over the next 180 or so years it seemed (to most Americans) that they couldn't go wrong by purchasing home. Housing was deemed a laudable public goal: If the man and woman on the street owned their homes, they wouldn't burn down their neighborhood. Revolts would be kept to a minimum. The peasants would be happy, which means the king is happy. Americans were marketed to by home builders and lenders. The message was clear: Buy a home. You'll make money. It's the best investment you'll ever make. Plus, you'll have a place to hang your hat at night and play ball with your kids.

Since the Great Depression of the 1930s housing was a safe bet. Home prices—on a national average—didn't decline. It was something that wasn't in the realm of the possible. There were regional implosions of home values—like during the oil bust of the 1980s—but in the general scheme of things these down cycles turned out to be minor hiccups that worked themselves out as local economies recovered, employment picked up, and people began looking at houses again. When enough lookers turned into buyers, homes prices would snap back to their pre-crash/correction levels. The regional down cycle had ended. Over the past 50 years it was more likely that an asteroid would hit the Earth than that home values would decline. Two ideas permeated the American psyche when it came to buying a home: (1) Real estate—God's not making any more of it. (2) The American dream cliché—housing is sacred, right up there with Mom, apple pie, and Chevy trucks.

Roughly $1.2 trillion later, owning a home no longer seems like such a smart idea. As we find ourselves on the precipice of a second Great Depression caused by the mortgage/housing/credit crisis, the math shakes out like this: $700 billion in taxpayer money allocated to buy troubled mortgages and mortgage-backed securities (MBSs) from lenders (including what's left of Wall Street), with some of the money being used for the bank nationalization plan. Add that to the $500 billion in losses already incurred by financial institutions (banks, S&Ls, Wall Street, insurance companies—take your pick) and you get $1.2 trillion.

If you're looking for the short version of how this crisis came about, it reads like this: The housing and mortgages bust was an economic bubble caused by Wall Street. In its thirst for profits, investment banking firms such as Bear Stearns, Merrill Lynch, and Lehman Brothers—the big three of the crisis—wanted to create bonds backed by mortgages so they could sell them to institutional investors in the United States and overseas. Institutional investors meant insurance companies, pension funds, banks, even state and local governments. All these clients were chasing yield (a greater return on their investment). For 30 years Wall Street had bought and packaged home mortgages into bonds; but these were primarily A credit quality loans—that is, mortgages made to consumers with good credit. Fannie Mae and Freddie Mac, two congressionally chartered mortgage investing giants, put their guarantee (their insurance) on these A paper mortgage bonds, which are called mortgage-backed securities (MBSs). The system functioned fine for three decades.

But Wall Street needed something more than "A" paper backed bonds to sell their customers. The Street turned to subprime mortgages because they carried a higher interest rate (2 percent to 3 percent more than A paper loans), which meant the bonds they created from such mortgages carried a higher yield. That's what Wall Street does; it sells stuff—stocks and bonds. An extra 2 percent to 3 percent yield on a $100 million subprime bond translates into millions of dollars in extra income for the investor. But aren't subprime mortgages, and therefore the bonds created from them, risky because the underlying loans are made to people with bad credit? Well, sure; but Wall Street bought bond insurance to protect investors and received top ratings (AAA) from firms like Standard & Poor's, Fitch, and Moody's. The three rating agencies were not exactly tough on Wall Street, because the bonds the Street firms were issuing had insurance, which meant if they went bad the investor would get paid off. The Street firms paid for the ratings they received, and if, for example, Fitch was too tough on, say, Merrill Lynch, Merrill would just go across the street to S&P. There was one core basic belief: that these subprime bonds would be fine because even if the mortgages went bad home prices would keep rising and the mortgage company and bond investor would get most of their money back. It turns out the Street firms barely looked at the quality of the subprime mortgages they were buying and securitizing; it was all outsourced to third parties.

Complicating the whole mess was the existence of another Wall Street product: the credit default swap (CDS). A swap, as noted earlier, is an insurance contract where an investor makes a bet against the value of a bond (a subprime bond, for instance, although the bet can be against any kind of bond). It's a totally unregulated business where insurance companies—and Wall Street firms—wrote insurance against billions of dollars' worth of subprime bonds that were issued from 2003 to early 2008, a period in which $2.6 trillion in subprime mortgages were originated to Americans. Most of those loans were packaged into bonds, mortgage-backed securities (MBSs) or asset-backed securities (ABSs). (Asset-backed securities is the term used to distinguish subprime-backed mortgage bonds from A paper credit quality mortgages.) No one seems entirely sure about the size of the credit default swap market, but the figure that keeps popping up is $44 trillion, which means if every single bond that has been bet against goes bad, whichever firm is on the hook for that insurance has to pay up. That's why we have a credit crisis.

I mention this brief history for one important reason: The $700 billion that you (the taxpayer) are funding will be used, at the very least, to buy subprime bonds from financial institutions. Even though $2.6 trillion in subprime mortgages were originated to Americans between 2003 and 2008, there are now roughly $1 trillion in these loans left in existence, the reason being that lenders constantly refinanced their own customers. (It was all about selling a product, the mortgage.) But the government won't be buying just subprime bonds. The new law opens up the floodgates for the U.S. Treasury to purchase any type of delinquent mortgage (and the bonds made from them), including alt-A mortgages (similar to subprime but the customer had a higher credit rating), payment option ARMs (also called the "I'll cry tomorrow" mortgage because to keep monthly payments low homeowners have the option of adding on to their actual debt), and even home equity loans or second liens. And as Mr. Lazear confirmed on the White House lawn that afternoon—don't rule out the government buying auto loans and credit card debt, too.

KEY ISSUE

One part of the legislation that hasn't received much publicity is that even though the bailout bill says the government will buy troubled assets to help alleviate the credit crisis, the word *troubled* is never defined, which means banks could potentially sell any type of mortgage, bond, or investment to Uncle Sam.

In mid-October the Treasury made it clear that it would also use the money to buy stakes in banks—which means these lenders have been partly nationalized. (In some quarters it's called socialism.) As Mr. Lazear told CNBC's Maria Bartiromo, "I don't like the idea of the government investing in stocks." Doing so went against what Republicans believed in—the free market. Mr. Lazear said in a dry tone, "The goal is not to make money on these stocks." But the government made the investment anyway—to show the world that there is nothing to fear, that Uncle Sam is standing behind the banking system. And what better way to do that than by owning a piece of it?

The Bailout Bill: First, the Good News

The $700 billion Emergency Economic Stabilization Act of 2008 (EESA), signed into law by President Bush on a sunny Friday afternoon in early October, provides no direct money to the consumer—but that doesn't mean the consumer will not ultimately benefit. The $700 billion will actually aid the struggling buyer, but it's going to take time—and yes, it's a bit complicated. As the Watergate source Deep Throat once advised investigative reporter Bob Woodward: follow the money.

As I noted in the Author's Note and Introduction of this book, the EESA legislation is somewhat akin to the Patriot Act in that the language of this bill (all 451 pages) is so vague—and it was passed with little serious debate in Congress (and in near record time)—that the government can pretty much act as it likes. Conspiracy theorists who believe in such concepts as the "Trilateral Commission" and a second shooter on the grassy knoll in Dallas are going to have a field day once they wake up and actually read the bill—which is now the law of the land. The partial nationalization of the banking system that occurred in mid-October may be just the beginning.

Under the EESA, the government can even bail out bankrupt towns, cities, and counties that have been hurt by the crisis. (Senators and members of Congress who want to help the voters back home should be extra nice to the Treasury secretary.) Some municipalities were hurt by buying bonds backed by subprime mortgages sold to them by salespeople on Wall Street, including Merrill Lynch. Here is a small sample of language (now law) that could, potentially, cost a bucket load of money: The Treasury Department can (to promote what's called "stability") come to the financial aid of what Congress (and the White House) calls "public instrumentalities." That would be towns and cities. (If you don't believe it, take a look at the excerpt from the bill that has been conveniently reprinted at the back of the book.)

But there's more. EESA also allows the Treasury Department to protect what it calls the "retirement security" of Americans. The government aims to do this buy purchasing troubled assets (again, subprime-backed mortgage bonds) from retirement plans. You may want to check the fine print of your 401(k) plan to see if your fund was unlucky (or dumb) enough to buy mortgage bonds backed by subprime loans. Another strain of horrible investments is the collateralized debt obligation (CDO), which is actually a bond made up of other bonds—in this case subprime bonds. Again, what is a bond? A bond is a security or investment that yields cash flow to the owner. Mortgage bonds are made up of (collateralized by) thousands upon thousands of mortgages or what are deemed whole loans.

A whole loan is industry jargon for the actual underlying mortgage. Most homeowners don't realize it, but after they take out a mortgage, the underlying whole loan is sold (usually immediately) into what's called the secondary market. The lender then retains the servicing rights on the loan, which means it receives a service fee for carrying out all the monthly processing work on the mortgage, that is, passing on the principal, interest, and real estate taxes to the proper parties. On a mortgage that carries an interest rate of, say, 6.25 percent, the 6 percent piece gets sold into the secondary market and the 0.25 percent is retained by the servicer, which continues to make money on the loan even though it has been sold into the nether-world of the financial services industry. Where that mortgage actually resides and who owns it is a chapter in itself. Suffice to say the modern world of housing finance—the one that is currently in ruins—has come a long way from the simple days of the Bailey Building and Loan.

In the old days (pre-1985), most mortgage lenders kept the loans they made. The deed of trust (mortgage) didn't disappear into the ether. It was down the block, resting in the file cabinet of your neighborhood savings and loan or bank. The secondary market is a fancy way of saying "your loan has been sold to someone else." That someone else often is Fannie Mae or Freddie Mac—the two large government-chartered companies whose mission is to buy mortgages from lenders, thus replenishing the pool of available mortgage money for consumers—or Wall Street, which, until this crisis reared its head, bought subprime loans. Fannie and Freddie—once privately held shareholder-owned corporations—are now wards of the government. They ran into financial trouble because they bought too many subprime bonds from Wall Street. At last count the two companies together owned $180 billion in subprime bonds or about 18 percent of all the A– to D quality mortgages in the United States.

Didn't Fannie and Freddie play a role in this crisis? The Republicans seem to blame them for the mess.

Answer: Fannie and Freddie played a role, to some degree, by purchasing so many subprime bonds from Wall Street. It can be argued that they set the table, but the two have countered that the bonds they bought were of the highest quality because they were AAA rated by rating agencies like S&P and Moody's. We know now that those ratings were worthless. Would the subprime business have grown so large without Fannie and Freddie buying the bonds? It can be argued that Wall Street could point to Fannie and Freddie's involvement in the market and say, "Look, Fannie and Freddie are buying subprime bonds. They must be a safe investment."

Bottom line: Fannie and Freddie did not invent the subprime mortgage or bond. Like other investors, they were looking for yield, and were subject to the same sales pitches Merrill Lynch gave to its other clients. The two believed their investments were safe. They were wrong. By purchasing subprime assets the two set an example for other investors.

The EESA bailout bill carries a few other hidden details that could, in theory, allow the federal government to pull out its checkbook and start bailing—that is, providing money. Here are two more that might catch the ire of the American public, depending on how they are spun:

1. **It's not just residential mortgages that the EESA bill rescues.** If the Treasury Department so desires, it can purchase apartment building loans* from troubled banks and S&Ls. And the

---

*In the world of banking and finance, apartment building loans are often referred to as "multifamily mortgages."

government's authority doesn't stop there. If the bank or S&L foreclosed on an apartment building owner, taking possession of the property, Uncle Sam can buy the building, too. This potentially makes the government a landlord, at least for a little while until the apartment project is sold.

It's not likely the government will end up owning too many apartment buildings, because this part of the housing market was not overbuilt. But as consumers lose their homes they will need somewhere to live, and that means apartment buildings. If enough Americans flock to rentals in cities, it could force rents up, depending on how many apartments are available for rent. But there is an upside on rentals in suburban areas: Whoever ends up owning those vacant single-family properties will not want to leave them empty. Investors who own them will want to get bodies in there, and in markets like Las Vegas that are extremely overbuilt, renting a vacant home might become quite cheap, especially in new subdivisions that are less than three years old.

2. **Preferred stock investments in Fannie Mae and Freddie Mac.** EESA doesn't come to the relief of individual investors who were unlucky enough to have bought preferred stock in Fannie and Freddie. (Preferred stock is different from common stock and in general carries a higher yield and other benefits.) Chances are if you own preferred shares in these two government-sponsored enterprises (GSEs) you're a wealthy individual who was probably talked into the investment by your stockbroker. Here, individuals are not in line for a bailout; but banks, S&Ls, and credit unions that own Fannie/Freddie preferred could receive a government handout if they have on-balance-sheet assets of less than $1 billion and were deemed "adequately capitalized" (had enough cash on hand) by their regulator as of June 30, 2008. EESA singles out banks that service working-class Americans, but there is nothing in the bill that rules out assistance to banks that serve wealthy communities and that have bought preferred stock in Fannie and Freddie.

Call Up Your Lender and Shout, "I Want to Restructure My Mortgage!"

In early 2007, when borrowers first began having trouble making their mortgage payments—in particular on adjustable rate mortgages (ARMs) that were resetting upward at a higher rate—a handful of lenders began creating specialized loan departments and dedicating staff to help struggling consumers. It was a small effort that didn't receive much notice in the media. Countrywide Home Loans—whose founder and former CEO Angelo Mozilo became something of the poster child of what was then mostly a mortgage crisis—was one of the first servicers to work with delinquent homeowners. Countrywide almost failed but was rescued by Bank of America, which took control of the lender in July 2008.

Don't get me wrong—when it came to foreclosures Mozilo's Countrywide was no angel of a lender. Prior to getting religion, it heaped on fees to delinquent borrowers who were late in paying their mortgages. Hint: In the world of mortgages and banking making fee income is what it's all about. Banks love to charge fees—especially late fees of any kind. (Remember your last credit card payment, the one you forgot to mail or click, and you wound up paying an extra $20, $30, or more?) Countrywide's foreclosure practices are still the subject of investigations in several states. I highlight the company because it was one of the first to work with borrowers, but its approach was an almost comical catch-22 that went something like this: Borrowers couldn't ask for assistance from Countrywide until they actually became late on their mortgage. In other words, even if a customer knew that he or she was going to have trouble making the higher loan payment when the adjustable rate mortgage went up, Countrywide wouldn't even entertain the thought of restructuring or modifying the loan until the borrower was actually late.

EESA is beneficial to delinquent or potentially delinquent homeowners on several fronts. By using billions of dollars to buy troubled mortgage-backed bonds, the government becomes the de facto owner of the underlying whole loan—which means that Uncle Sam can at his will rewrite bad home mortgages to save a borrower from foreclosure. The bill even says the Treasury secretary will use "loan guarantees" and "credit enhancements" to facilitate the rewriting of delinquent mortgages to "prevent avoidable" foreclosures. These phrases might sound like Latin to the typical consumer, but basically they mean the government will rewrite loans that are worth saving by reducing the loan amount and writing a brand-new mortgage insured by the government's own mortgage insurance company, the Federal Housing Administration (FHA).

It's unclear how heavy a hand Treasury will use to restructure delinquent home mortgages. Some of it will depend on the unemployment situation of the borrower and whether rewriting the loan—giving the borrower a new lower rate or reduced loan balance—will make a difference. In some cases the government might decide that the borrower is so late in his or her payments that a lower rate or loan amount won't make much difference over the long haul.

One fact should be pointed out to consumers: Whether they realize it or not, foreclosing on a home can be costly to the servicer whose job it is to collect the monthly payments. Depending on where the foreclosure takes place, the legal processing alone of foreclosing can cost anywhere from $15,000 to $20,000 on up, and that doesn't even factor in all the lost monthly payments the servicer must eat. Note: Some states, like Maryland, have put a moratorium on foreclosures—but these cooling-off periods have expiration dates.

KEY ISSUE

One route the government may take in buying all of those billions of dollars' worth of troubled mortgage securities is deconstructing the security—that is, breaking it apart into thousands of whole loans. The Treasury Department, since it will own those loans, can rewrite any of them—meaning delinquent borrowers could see their loan amount or interest rate, or both, reduced.

Before EESA was even a spark of a thought in the mind of Treasury secretary Henry Paulson, a dozen or so residential lenders/servicers had formed a group of their own—the HOPE NOW alliance—to help rewrite delinquent loans. By November 2008, HOPE NOW boasted 27 participating mortgage companies, including all of the largest residential servicers, which include what now might be deemed the big four of the U.S. mortgage market: Bank of America (which includes the Countrywide franchise); CitiMortgage (part of the Citigroup financial services empire); Wells Fargo & Company; and Chase Home Finance (part of bank/investment bank powerhouse JPMorgan Chase). The following table details just how much these four control the home loan business:

Servicer Rank	Company Name	Amount of Home Loans Serviced	Market Share of Home Loan Business
1	Bank of America	$2.025 trillion	21.06%
2	CitiMortgage	1.519 trillion	15.82
3	Wells Fargo	1.496 trillion	15.56
4	Chase Home Finance	829 billion	8.62
Total		**$5.166 trillion**	**61.06%**

Source: National Mortgage News.
Note: The market share is calculated by taking the dollar amount of outstanding home mortgages in the United States ($9.6 trillion) and dividing it by each lender's portfolio of home mortgages that it services each month.

Fifteen years ago it was unheard-of for just one servicer to control more than 5 percent of the home mortgage market. As of late 2008 the big four (let's hope they don't wind up like the "Big Three" automakers) control 61 percent of all the home mortgages in the nation, including second liens and home equity lines of credit (HELOCs).

Therefore, a basic question that consumers and our elected leaders face is: Are Bank of America, CitiMortgage, Wells Fargo, and Chase too big to fail—just the way Fannie Mae and Freddie Mac were? There is a new definition for liquidity in the United States (as it applies to companies, including banks), and it goes something like this: A business is liquid (solvent) as long as investors are willing to lend money to it. It's that simple. In the case of financial institutions like Bank of America, Citigroup, and the rest of the nation's largest deposit takers, their lenders are consumers whose deposits rest in their bank vaults. When many customers decide to pull out all their money at once, that's what we call a run on the bank.

THE UGLY FACTS

- There are roughly 58.3 million outstanding mortgages in the United States. About 9 percent of them are delinquent, an all-time high.
- About 35 percent of all subprime loans ($1 trillion in outstanding balances) are late, which translates into $350 billion.
- Of the nation's $9.6 trillion in residential loans, about 1.5 percent are in some stage of foreclosure—which means millions of consumers are in danger of losing their homes.

The HOPE NOW alliance likes to tout the fact that it has prevented 2.07 million loans from going into foreclosure since its members started their rescue efforts in the summer of 2007. On the surface the figure sounds impressive, but is it? I interviewed Faith Schwartz, who serves as executive director of the alliance, about the foreclosure relief efforts of her organization. Keep in mind there are two ways to help struggling borrowers with their home mortgages. The first is to create a repayment plan that helps the customer make up missed monthly payments. In this case the dollar amount of the mortgage stays the same. The other way to fix a bad loan is to engage in a loan modification where the dollar amount owed is permanently lowered. So, what's the dollar amount of money HOPE NOW's members have saved delinquent homeowners? Ms. Schwartz doesn't know.

Another question for the alliance was this: Okay, so you've helped fix up 2.07 million loans (out of a total universe of 58.3 million mortgages in the United States); how many of those fixed-up loans have slipped back into delinquency? Faith—who used to work at Freddie Mac as well as a now-defunct subprime lender called Option One Mortgage—didn't know the answer to that one, either. Helping people avoid losing their homes is a laudable goal, but until HOPE NOW can provide more detailed figures on its results, Americans shouldn't be fooled by all the bullet points contained in the group's press releases. The bottom line is this: If you're in danger of losing your home, the EESA bill will help. The old Countrywide edict of "you have to be late on your payments before we can help you" is now out the window. Mortgage companies (servicers) are willing to cut deals. Dial the 800 number on your mortgage payment stub and ask them. If the customer service rep (who might actually be located in India) seems unwilling to hear your plea, ask for the manager. If the company is still unwilling to deal, dial the HOPE NOW alliance. Its phone number is: (888) 995-HOPE. If the alliance seems unwilling to help, call your member of Congress or local television station. The nation's foreclosure and credit crisis is a story that's not going away.

HOPE NOW alliance's members include, among others:

- Bank of America
- Chase Home Finance
- CitiMortgage
- HSBC Bank
- National City
- Saxon Mortgage
- SunTrust Mortgage
- Wells Fargo

The Bad News: Getting a Mortgage
Is Going to Be Much Tougher

The EESA legislation might also be called the "Trickle-Down Help" bill. By buying bad mortgage bonds, the government can restructure loans by reducing the loan amount and interest rate for the consumer. The Treasury can force lenders to do the same. I've already gone over this turf a bit, but what if you're a new mortgage customer and want to buy a house? This is where it gets tricky. A few stark facts of the new lending landscape are taking shape:

- **The days of easy credit are over.** You'll need a good credit score to get a loan. If you don't know your credit score, ask your current lender (if you have one) or go online and find out. If you don't even know what a credit score is, you're in trouble. (It's a grade of your financial ability to repay debt based on your past history of bill payments.)
- **Cash is king.** Even if you have a good credit score, you'll need a down payment. The only refuge for people with 3 percent or less to put down will be the aforementioned FHA program, which is insurance written by the government. Private mortgage insurance companies like Genworth, MGIC Investment Group, and the PMI Group are under extreme financial pressure because they're having to make good on all the policies written during the boom years. (There are just seven private-sector mortgage insurance companies.) Mortgage insurance companies are already cutting way back on who they cover. At present, if a lender like, say, Bank of America is originating your loan and then selling it to Fannie Mae and Freddie Mac (the secondary market), you will need private mortgage insurance unless you can muster a down payment of at least 20 percent.

KEY ISSUE

> Mortgage insurance companies are beginning to make severe changes in what types of loans they will cover. Radian, a mortgage insurer based in Philadelphia, will not insure condominiums in some areas of Florida and most of Nevada. In the fall of 2008 it declared that it would no longer insure any condo loan if it was originated by a third-party loan broker. (Brokers are intermediaries that act as freelance salespeople for bigger lenders like Bank of America and Wells Fargo.)

- **Down payment assistance programs have been banned by the government.** A year ago 79,000 people used down payment assistance (DPA) plans to purchase homes, most of them in new developments. The process worked like this: A nonprofit like the Nehemiah Corporation of California would give down payment money to a home buyer. The seller (a home building company, usually) would then reimburse the nonprofit and pay a fee for the service. But to make its profit margins, it is believed that the seller (the home builder) would just jack up the price enough to cover the reimbursement to the nonprofit. The government shut down the program because it found mortgages made with DPA money went bad much faster than transactions where there was none.

- **You will need to verify your current employment situation and the deposits you have in your bank account.** You can no longer just state your income and expect the lender to believe you. (These were called stated-income or liar loans.) If you're self-employed, round up your income tax filings from the previous three years. Some lenders may require five years of returns.

• **We are now a consolidation nation.** With so many lenders
going bust the past 18 months (about 400 at last check, and that
doesn't include the number of laid-off loan brokers), the actual
number of firms willing to even make a loan has been depleted.
The top four mortgage gorillas mentioned earlier—Bank of
America, CitiMortgage, Wells Fargo, and Chase Home Finance—
now control six of every ten loans originated. Never before have
so few controlled so much of the home lending business in this
nation. With credit unions going under almost as fast as banks, consumers will have less choice when it comes to mortgages, credit
cards, and other financial instruments. Less choice is generally not
a good thing when it comes to shopping for anything, in particular
financial products.

Now that these banks have been partly nationalized, rest assured
they are not going away. They could grow even bigger as Uncle Sam
tries to merge (dump) ailing banks into their companies.

The final irony: The subprime lending business—where $800 bil-
lion a year in loans were written (in the best year)—has been wiped
off the map. There are about 10 lenders left from a onetime total
of 250. Thanks to the economic carnage of the past year, there will be
more potential subprime borrowers than ever before. But no one will
lend to them.

A Word about Interest Rates

Predicting interest rates is a fool's game. I've sat through enough economic forecast conferences that I can let you in on a secret: Most of
the predictions I've heard—with some exceptions—turn out wrong.
Few economists make any radical forecasts about rates rising and
falling, opting instead to make predictions where changes in interest rates or home construction are gradual. Economists are flawed
professionals, and they know it. But they're also very good at telling

jokes to make their audience forget how bad their forecast was the prior year.

I like economists, though. And I enjoy attending their crystal ball sessions, particularly the fall and spring forecast shows held by the National Association of Home Builders (NAHB) at their headquarters in Washington, D.C. The NAHB is one of the powerful lobbying organizations in the United States. It is effective politically because of this stark fact: Its members donate a ton of money to members of Congress, senators, and presidential candidates, arguing that housing is good for the country and the economy. It's a potent argument. Plus, in Washington money talks. A friend who used to work there explained NAHB's philosophy to me: "They candy coat everything so people will go out and keep buying houses and their members keep paying their dues."

I'm no economist, but it's tempting—after attending enough of those forecast shows—to take a stab at telling you where mortgage rates might be headed. So here goes. Mortgages could fall to as low as 5 percent by the end of 2009. But there's a caveat: This is only for borrowers with a pristine credit history. If you have good credit with a personal FICO score north of 700 and you can muster a down payment of 10 percent (although 20 percent may become the norm), you should have no trouble getting a loan. However, if you don't have pristine credit, you will pay more for your mortgage—in terms of the rate charged or points on the loan. (One point or 1 percent of a $100,000 mortgage works out to $1,000 payable at the closing table.) This is already happening. Also, if you have a higher loan-to-value (LTV) ratio you will pay more. The key will be down payment money. You will need at least 20 percent—and a higher FICO score—to avoid the higher charges. If you don't want to pay the higher charges, then you won't get a mortgage. (If you obtain a mortgage with 20 percent down, that means you have a LTV ratio of 80 percent.)

So how come rates will fall? Isn't the United States in deep financial trouble with the $10.3 trillion in debt it owes on all its borrowings, plus being on the hook (if something should go wrong) with Fannie and Freddie, which adds another $5 trillion? You would think that our lenders (investors who buy Treasury securities) would shy away from buying our bonds, which means we'd have to increase the interest rate on them (to entice buyers back). If Treasury rates rise, so too will mortgage rates. But now that Europe and Asia have caught our sub-prime flu, the United States—as hard as it is to fathom—is still seen as a safe haven.

Now say a prayer.

Falling Home Values

The biggest piece of bad news is the most obvious: Home values will not recover anytime soon, and in certain once-hot markets like Arizona, California, Florida, and Nevada, homes bought during the go-go years of 2004 to early 2007 could lose up to 50 percent of their value. Too many home buyers who shouldn't have been allowed to buy homes (because they had no down payments or their credit was bad) received mortgages.

We, as a nation, are in the middle of a housing bubble. Bubbles take time to work out. Two economic factors drive home purchases: interest rates (which will continue to be low) and employment. Employment is key.

Which cities in particular face the toughest sledding over the next two years? The PMI Group is a publicly traded mortgage insurance company based in San Francisco. Its mission in life—besides trying to make money for its shareholders—is covering losses on mortgages funded by banks, savings and loans (S&Ls), and mortgage companies. If a mortgage goes south, PMI will pay up to 20 percent of the losses. What is interesting about the concept is that the insurance policy is paid for by the consumer as part of his or her monthly payment, but the policy covers (part of) the lender's losses on the note!

PMI recently conducted a study on which cities—known as metropolitan statistical areas (MSAs)—are at the most risk of seeing more of their citizens' mortgages go bad. It looked at home prices, foreclosure rates, and employment. The company's theory is simple: As foreclosures rise home prices will fall. It found 16 cities/MSAs that it deemed high-risk in regard to suffering a protracted decline in values. Eight of the cities are in California, which accounts for 20 percent of the entire mortgage market. Five are in Florida, with one each in Arizona, Nevada, and Rhode Island. Here are the top 10:

1. Fort Lauderdale/Pompano Beach/Deerfield Beach, Florida
2. Riverside/San Bernardino/Ontario, California
3. Orlando/Kissimmee, Florida
4. Miami/Miami Beach/Kendall, Florida
5. Tampa–St. Petersburg/Clearwater, Florida
6. Las Vegas/Paradise, Nevada
7. Los Angeles/Long Beach/Glendale, California
8. Santa Ana/Anaheim/Irvine, California (Note: Most of the nation's largest subprime lenders were headquartered in Orange County or in surrounding areas.)
9. Jacksonville, Florida
10. Phoenix/Mesa/Scottsdale, Arizona

The Wealthy Will Not Escape Unscathed

If you think the so-called rich will survive this real estate downturn, you're mistaken. The toughest loans that consumers might have a hard time getting are those where the amount is north of $729,750. Why this number? This is the Fannie Mae and Freddie Mac loan limit cap. They cannot buy mortgages greater than this amount. Lenders sell their loans (now, more than ever) to Fannie and Freddie. (It doesn't matter that Fannie and Freddie are owned by Uncle Sam.) If a lender cannot sell the loan, it might keep it on its books—or avoid making such a large loan (which is called a "super jumbo" mortgage) altogether. But very few lenders are willing to touch these loans anymore, because of the credit crisis. This could hammer the homes that sell north of $729,750. (Note: As per the bailout bill, the Fannie/Freddie loan limit drops to $650,000 in 2009, so the impact could be even greater.)

Mike Covino, a mortgage banker based in Tarrytown, New York, less than 30 miles from Manhattan, sees no upside for the super jumbo market under the $700 billion bailout plan. "If you cut off funding for anything, it dies," he told me. A lender for almost 30 years, he fears home prices in the greater New York area could go into a free fall the next few years, some falling by as much as 30 percent. He fears for such areas as Greenwich and Fairfield in Connecticut, and all of Westchester. From a political standpoint, helping consumers who fall in the super jumbo loan category is tricky. It falls into the "no bailout for Wall Street" camp. "No one is going to stand up for them," he said. He's right.

The Silver Lining: Falling Home Prices Mean Bargains for Some

Home prices, on average, are going to fall over the next two years, at least. No doubt about it. The last thing in the world a bank wants to do is hold on to a house it has foreclosed on. That means auctions. Banks, savings and loans, and credit unions across the nation—in particular those operating in neighborhoods hardest hit by the housing bubble— are going to move to sell their inventory (foreclosed homes) as quickly as possible. Take the case of Trisha Bayles of Maryland. In early October 2008, she bought a two-story brick home in suburban Laurel (about 15 miles from the nation's capital) for $200,000. To some people living in rural America $200,000 might seem like a lot of money. But a year earlier, according to a story in the *Washington Post*, the same house had sold for $465,000—a stunning price decline of 57 percent. Bayles, by the way, signed a contract to buy the house by making a $23,000 down payment or 11.5 percent of the purchase price. Strong down payments are going to be the norm—whether you're buying at a foreclosure auction or not.

During the height of savings and loan crisis (1989–1994) the government bailout agency in change of the cleanup—the Resolution Trust Corporation (RTC)—held what might be viewed as the nation's greatest garage sale ever. Each year the government, employing private-sector real estate auction companies, sold 200,000 units of housing—single-family dwellings and condominiums. Uncle Sam, which closed roughly 1,000 S&Ls and banks during that downturn, also held "everything must go" sales of all the furnishings inside these bankrupt institutions. Quite a few banks and thrifts (thrift is another word for S&L) also owned cars (to shuttle employees around); planes (to shuttle executives around); and all the tools of the trade: computers, copiers, desks, office furniture, and even expensive artwork. All of it was sold to the public, who found bargains in the scrap heap of the S&L industry.

This time around, Americans will not be facing the same government-sponsored garage sale. The mandate of the $700 billion bailout bill is to buy troubled mortgages and mortgage-backed bonds from financial institutions. Uncle Sam hopes he won't be liquidating furniture and computers from dozens of failed banks. Then again, S&Ls and banks have failed and will continue to go bust. If the government can't find a buyer (another bank) for the branches and headquarters, it will hire auction companies to clear out buildings, which means consumers could benefit from these office sales. Auctions are usually advertised in the local newspaper or on the cable channel. If you need a couch, check your listings.

How Will We Know When Home Prices Have Stopped Falling?

Predicting when home values will bottom out is right up there in terms of foolishness with making forecasts on interest rates. How many times during the housing boom do you remember sitting around with your neighbors having a beer or coffee, asking these two questions: "How can they pay so much for that place?" and "Who's buying these houses?" To some of us living in New York, California, Las Vegas, or the greater Washington, D.C., area, the stellar increases each year seemed unfathomable. Some of us had a sinking feeling that it wouldn't last. Well, it didn't.

Back in 2005—a record year for subprime lending in the United States ($810 billion or 25 percent of all loans)—roughly 42 percent of all new homes purchased were purchased without a down payment, which means these home buyers had nothing to lose. They had "no skin in the game." If their employment situation went south, they could walk away without worrying about losing their down payment or equity, because there was none.

Home prices will begin to rise again only when the unemployment rate improves markedly and consumers feel good about their job stability. The other key ingredient is interest rates, which I've already talked about. I do have one theory about home prices, though, and it works like this: Check local rents for apartments and homes, especially for two and three bedrooms. Compare the price to what it would take buy a three-bedroom house by factoring in a modest down payment of 10 percent. Your comparison should be apples to apples. If you're looking at a house in a certain neighborhood in Brooklyn, see what rentals go for in that neighborhood. Compare the monthly cost to rent versus paying a mortgage. If the rental is much cheaper than buying, that's your answer on a recovery. When all the numbers are punched in and the calculations made, the reality for home prices may look quite bleak.

Chapter 3

Where to Put Your Money Now

(Hint: Not in a Vacation Home)

"Cash is king."

—ANCIENT FINANCIAL PROVERB

The downturn in the economy caused by the mortgage and credit crisis has affected all sorts of investments—from stocks and bonds to cash, commodities, and real estate—that will impact your current financial situation as well as your retirement down the road. Yet it seems that the decline in home values is at the center of this crisis, affecting the underlying mortgages and the bonds created from them.

It is in the hearth where most Americans have their wealth: their residence. But the carnage also will harm the second home and vacation market, an area that has yet to receive much media attention primarily because the impact on it hasn't happened yet. But it's coming. Luckily for owners of vacation homes, the summer rental season ended before the stock market crashed. Next summer could be an entirely different story as renters stay away, affecting the ability of landlords to pay their mortgages. This could be the other shoe to drop, which is why it deserves more attention.

Realtors—those seemingly kind people whose job it is to sell us houses—are eternal optimists. In an economic downturn like what we're in now, don't believe a word they say. They want you to buy. Their commission depends on it. If you're looking at a home or vacation getaway at the beach or in the mountains, bid low, very low. Don't for a minute buy what the Realtor says about the property's value and rental history. By law a Realtor has to submit your offer to the home-owner. These are challenging times. If you bought a vacation property over the past three years with very little money down, you could be facing a potential financial crisis—that is, if you're dependent on rental income to pay the mortgage.

That said, here's a little story about the state of the vacation home market: A friend of mine who works in the mortgage insur-ance industry—and who likes to keep his name out of newspapers and books—took his wife to Duck, North Carolina, for a birthday/getaway weekend. It was right before the stock market crashed. Duck is located on the Outer Banks. It's a strip of land on the Atlantic Ocean that has been attracting vacationers for 50 years. The area began to boom 20 years ago. In time, like any piece of land located on or near water, Duck began to get pricey, with 5,000-square-foot oceanfront homes boasting six bedrooms (for big family get-togethers) selling for well over $1.5 million. Smaller properties located off the beach or condos on the bay side might sell for $500,000 to a $1 million.

In early October 2008, my friend was driving down Highway 12 heading home to Raleigh from Duck. His wife took the wheel and he began to count the number of For Sale signs littering the landscape. After 15 minutes, he stopped counting; 47 homes located on the main drag (Highway 12) were up for sale. And these were only the homes he could see from the road—and at night (he wears glasses—bifocals). The year-round population of Duck is a little over 700. He later discovered that three realty firms had set up business on the barrier island to handle nothing but sales of foreclosed properties. He didn't even bother counting the For Sale signs in nearby Kitty Hawk. It was getting late and he was tired of counting.

Back in 2005 the National Association of Realtors (NAR), a trade organization that represents 1.2 million men and women who sell homes, released a study that made headlines in the financial press. The group found that second homes—primarily vacation and investment properties—accounted for 36 percent of all home sales the year before. It was the first time ever NAR had conducted such a study. Its findings were derived from an eight-page survey it had mailed to 100,000 consumers who had bought a home the prior year. The research wasn't exactly deep, but on the surface proved interesting. Some members of the press concluded that baby boomers—that post–World War II demographic of 80 million—were doing to the vacation market what they had been doing to home prices for primary residences: driving up values. Boomers are an economic force unto themselves. If they all chase after the same thing at the same time, it goes up in value: supply and demand. God isn't making any more waterfront lots.

In case you didn't know, the vacation home market didn't exactly peter out in 2005. It grew stronger each year. And of course if a consumer wants to buy a vacation home he or she (or both) will need a mortgage. Just how many mortgages are originated each year that are used to fund either a vacation home or an investment property is unclear. Estimates range from 5 percent to 20 percent.

NAR officials—who always like to put a positive spin on the numbers—point out that the typical vacation home buyer is 55 years old with an annual income of $71,000, which translates into: don't worry. They also estimate that the median price (the halfway point between the highest and lowest value) of the typical vacation home sold in 2007 was just $195,000, a slight dip from the prior year. In other words, the message seems to be: don't panic—this market will be just fine. But my friend's recent trip to Duck suggests that things are not fine and this once very hot sector of the housing business could be headed for a steep fall. And as the house goes, so goes the mortgage. In the world of finance, it's all about cash flow, baby. If the vacation property investors can continue to rent it out to cover the mortgage or if they are wealthy enough to carry the unit without rental income, then they'll be okay.

It's everyone else I worry about. Investors with beach houses know they have 12 weeks to make as much money as they can to cover the mortgage: Memorial Day to Labor Day. Depending on the size of their mortgage (and their personal employment situation), missing a week or two could turn tragic.

One key bright spot: Even though prices for beach and mountain homes are falling (as are rental prices for some of these units), Americans have been so harmed by this economic downturn (stock market losses, higher fuel prices, unemployment or underemployment) that traveling to Europe is cost prohibitive. The U.S. dollar is been so weak the past five years (though it's making somewhat of a comeback) that its exchange rate against most European currencies has been abysmal. A neighbor of mine traveled to London on business in early 2008 and came back with stories of $60 lunches—and that was just his share. (Lunch did include a martini.) With Europe likely to stay expensive for the middle class—a suffering middle class, that is—Americans will stay home and rent at U.S. beaches. But you can anticipate that the renters will want a bargain. Then again, some might just skip the rental, stay home, and head for the local pool.

The Day the Flipping Stopped

A few months back I interviewed Jim Rokakis, the treasurer of Cuyahoga County, Ohio, which includes the city of Cleveland. Rokakis had spent some of his time investigating home foreclosures in the Cleveland area. In particular, he focused on a small inner-city hamlet called Slavic Village that was changing over from Polish and Czech immigrants to Hispanics and blacks. One subprime lender, Argent Mortgage, had done a brisk business in the area, originating 11,000 mortgages from 2003 to 2007. (A subprime lender, Argent was ultimately owned by Roland Arnall, a press-shy businessman who was also a large fund-raiser for President Bush.)

By late 2007, it had turned out that the homes Argent had funded during those years had total negative equity of $230 million, meaning that is how overvalued they were. Rokakis was steaming mad and began to kick some tires. He discovered that real estate speculators—thanks to mortgages arranged by Argent—had targeted Slavic Village. The idea was to buy a house as cheaply as possible and then flip it for several thousand dollars more. Slavic Village was not a vacation area, although the Rock and Roll Hall of Fame and Museum is within a 20-minute drive, depending on traffic. When the subprime crisis began to accelerate and many lenders failed or left the area, the speculators shied away and the flipping stopped. Foreclosures began to pile up. Rokakis and other city officials set up a program to help homeowners who were in danger of losing their houses. One young man who approached the county treasurer was late on seven mortgages. He wasn't living in all seven properties (obviously). He was a speculator. This young man had been playing the flipping game. Now he was caught without enough renters to cover his mortgages, and there was no one to whom he could flip the properties. He applied for the city's foreclosure program but was turned down. Rokakis—who loathed speculators for what they had done to the Slavic Village—wanted to choke him. "He was just a young kid, in his twenties," said Rokakis.

Joe Falk of Florida is a past president of the National Association of Mortgage Brokers, a trade group that represents independent salesmen and saleswomen who originate mortgages using money from other firms. Loan brokers have been tarred and feathered in connection in the subprime crisis because some of their banks were selling loans to consumers, knowing they probably couldn't pay them back. Some brokers have also been known to tack on junk fees and charges in an effort to increase their personal income on certain loans.

Falk knows there are both good and bad loan brokers out there, and he's happy to see the bad ones leave the business via unemployment and indictments. Nonetheless, he has to deal with the aftermath of the mortgage/credit crisis and Florida's ailing real estate market, believed to be one of the worst in the nation, right up there with California and Nevada in terms of price declines and foreclosures. He cited to me this one startling statistic for Dade County (which includes the city of Miami): 25,000 condominiums are for sale, and another 15,000 are under construction. But in September 2008 just 400 sold. Asked about the condos that are under construction, he said, "What are they going to do? Stop a 30-story building even if they're only on the 15th floor and leave the thing sitting unfinished?"

THE UGLY FACTS

Under the Emergency Economic Stabilization Act (EESA), the government may take control of a consumer's delinquent home mortgage and attempt to bring it current—even reduce the loan amount—but this is for owner-occupied mortgages only. In other words, if you're an investor who is delinquent on a vacation or second home you're out of luck.

Following is a sample of hot (and once-hot) vacation markets that could suffer over the next five years:

- Orlando, Florida
- Las Vegas, Nevada
- Duck, North Carolina
- The New Jersey shore
- The Hamptons
- Rehoboth, Delaware

- Cape Cod
- Lake Tahoe
- Vail, Colorado
- Fill in the blank yourself. Pick any beach, mountain, or other resort area where prices rose 20 percent from 2002 to 2007, and pencil it in.
- Ditto for time-shares.

Bottom line: Mickey Mouse isn't entirely recession proof. The Orlando condo market is among the worst in the nation in terms of units for sale and overbuilding. As for the Hamptons out on Long Island, this is Wall Street's summer playground. Wall Street is toast. The days of profligate investment bankers buying $6 ice cream cones at the gelato shop on Main Street could be over.

The Contrarian Play in Vacation Homes

Now that I've just depressed the hell out of you by predicting what a potential train wreck the vacation market could turn into, there's also the other side of the coin to consider. If the vacation market cracks up (and I think some resort areas will, depending on how high home and condo prices rose over the past five years), now could possibly be a time to bottom-fish. If you have the stomach for this game, here are a few things to consider:

- **Study the rental market where you're considering buying in.** Even with the economic downturn, what is the likelihood that you can get a steady flow of renters this summer (or ski season) to help cover your mortgage?
- **Be prepared to make a 20 percent down payment, maybe even 30 percent.** If you're eyeing a condo, some lenders won't

even make these loans anymore, especially if it's an investment property. And some mortgage insurance companies won't even write a policy to cover potential losses.

- **Bid low.** Think of Duck. An overabundance of sellers means bargains should abound for buyers. Get your financing arranged in advance so the seller knows you're serious.
- **If you know of a property that is in trouble but not yet foreclosed on, contact the bank.** Some banks will allow you to buy the house at a lower price directly from them (with the homeowner's approval) prior to foreclosure. This is called a short sale.

All delinquent mortgages will be handled by the government through the Troubled Asset Relief Program (TARP) created under EESA. But I have a sense that the Treasury Department hasn't thought about how many mortgages it will eventually own that are collateralized by vacation homes and investment properties. As a bottom-fisher, it may pay to wait until mid-2009 when Treasury gets into full swing. If the government winds up owning more loans backed by vacation homes, that could cause yet more downward pressure on prices in resort areas.

Investing in Foreclosures

Investing in foreclosed properties may seem easy, but it's not. You may have seen advertisements on cable TV or in the weekly *Pennysaver* about how you, too, can get rich by investing in foreclosed homes. Most of these come-on advertisements want to sell you a kit including software or a book. Chances are there might be classes or a seminar to attend at a local hotel. The cost: several hundred dollars. Beware the well-dressed huckster with slicked-back hair, promising you riches on late-night TV.

But that's not to say there aren't opportunities buying foreclosed properties. Don Henig is a former mortgage lender who worked on Long Island and lost his job when his company, American Home

Mortgage, went bust in the summer of 2007. (American Home was a nonbank lender that originated both A paper loans and alt-A mortgages.) After losing his job, Don, who had 20-plus years in the lending business, spent a year studying the Long Island foreclosure market. Henig did not have big dollar signs in his eyes. At first he was skeptical that he could buy homes at a low-enough price and then turn them around for sale at a decent profit.

He began buying slowly. During his first six months in operation he bought and sold 30 homes in the greater New York and New Jersey area. I don't know how profitable Don's operation is, but he quoted me one sale where he bought a home in Deer Park, Long Island, for $151,000, fixed it up, and then sold it for $375,000. (A few caveats about this story: Henig put up his own money but also found a venture capital partner. He then teamed up with another firm called Island Properties of Farmingdale that helps him rehabilitate some of the dilapidated homes he buys at foreclosure.)

Caution: This is not a business for novices. Foreclosure buying is not without risk. You'll need money to buy the homes and fix them up. If you don't have liquidity (someone available to lend you money), do not play in this arena.

Stocks: Is Now the Time to Get In?

In the fall of 2007 the stock market hit an all-time high of 14,280. Roughly 12 months later it was in a free fall. The selling, in earnest, came after the House of Representatives first rejected the $700 billion bailout package for the mortgage and credit markets on September 29, 2008. (That's when indignant consumers could be seen on television ranting, "I'm not going to bail out rich investment bankers on Wall Street.") Even after the bill eventually passed (loaded down with pork-barrel giveaways to sway certain votes in Congress) and the stock market breathed a small sigh of relief, the selling began again—down

400 points one day, up 200, down 700, up 50, down 600. By mid-October, when the worst of the selling seemed to be finished, investors had lost $8.4 trillion worth of wealth in the stock market.

I don't make my living giving out stock advice. I cover mortgages, real estate, and banking and the men and women who manage those businesses. I also don't invest in stocks I write about, namely banks and mortgage-related companies; but there are a few commonsense thoughts consumers should keep in mind about stock valuations. (This applies to both regular trading and 401(k) investments.)

Even after the $700 billion bailout bill was signed into law to help both lenders and homeowners get back on their feet, stocks continued to dive. By October 10, 2008, a Friday, the market had sold off 2,271 points during the previous seven sessions. The Dow Jones Industrial Average was down 42 percent from a year before. This is Great Depression territory, except this time around I don't remember seeing any stories about people jumping out of windows when their fortunes evaporated (probably because most modern office buildings are hermetically sealed, which means their tenants can't open the windows. If they want to jump, they'll have to go up to the roof.)

The natural inclination for many people is to look at the carnage and say, "The Dow is at 8,000. It was at 14,280 a year ago. That's cheap. I'm jumping in with both feet." Yes, in the fall of 2008 the market was off 42 percent, but investors should not rely on the stock index for an entry or reentry point into the market. If Dow 30 companies were posting strong earnings the previous two years and suddenly looked cheap because their stock price had crumbled 40 percent, that doesn't mean they *are* cheap! The economy of 2009 to 2011 will not be economy of 2006 to midyear 2008. These Dow 30 companies will not have the same earnings going forward. You cannot compare them. Just because Exxon posted $50 zillion in earnings those years doesn't mean it will post $50 zillion in earnings the next two years.

Economically speaking, we are in uncharted territory. Unemployment is rising, consumers who still have jobs are fearful of losing them, and the price of gasoline is still relatively high (though well below the nosebleed territory we saw in the summer of 2008 when it broke $4 a gallon). Even if gasoline continues to fall in price, families with kids won't be buying brand-new Chevy Tahoes anymore to cart their broods around. They'll opt for a small Toyota. There is a fear that even though the price of oil is falling again it could turn around at any time, heading north on a rocket.

KEY ISSUE

A company's stock can be considered cheap only if it has fallen significantly and its earnings going forward will be slightly better or stronger than in years past. If future earnings are expected to drop, then even a 43 percent decline in price cannot be considered cheap. When an investor buys a stock that has fallen in value because it appears cheap—only to see that stock head even lower—that's called "catching a falling knife."

When the stock market crashed in October, Merrill Lynch's chief investment strategist, Richard Bernstein (the go-to guy for bullish signals), penned a report to the company's clients entitled "Hard Times." Bernstein told investors there are four indicators the company will be watching going forward to judge a reentry point into the market: sentiment, valuation, earnings estimate revisions by companies, and the unemployment rate. He also pointed to what's called the "3 percent dividend yield rule," which suggests that investors should be bullish when the Standard & Poor's index of 500 select companies breaks through that level. (The dividend yield is calculated by taking into consideration the share price and quarterly dividends.) Merrill's Bernstein calculated that after the bloodbath of early October 2008 the dividend on the S&P 500 was 3.3 percent.

To his credit, Bernstein hinted that there was always a risk that publicly traded companies would cut dividends to preserve cash, which means that the attractive 3.3 percent dividend rate on the S&P 500 could fall, maybe significantly.

There is one thought to keep in mind about Merrill Lynch: It was a major player in the nation's subprime crisis. It not only financed many subprime mortgage lenders by lending them money, but it also bought those loans and packaged them into bonds, selling them overseas. Those very same bonds—which are now worth a lot less because the loans collateralizing them carry delinquency rates north of 30 percent—are at the heart of how the nation found itself in this financial mess.

Before the market crash, Merrill loved the subprime bond business so much that it went out and bought its own subprime lending company, First Franklin Financial Corporation of San Jose, California, paying $1.3 billion for the company and two affiliates. Merrill wanted to own a loan factory that was producing all those subprime mortgages so it would have an assured pipeline of mortgages to feed its bond sale business. It was all about selling bonds to its institutional customers, including state and local governments, corporations, and the same overseas. Merrill, like many Wall Street firms, was careless about the quality of subprime loans it was buying.

That's not to denigrate Bernstein. His research feeds Merrill's army of stock pickers. Before Merrill made the tragic decision to get involved in subprime, its forte was peddling stocks through its retail stockbrokers. When Merrill spoke, investors listened—not just in the United States but worldwide. During the financial meltdown in the fall, it looked as though Merrill too might fail; but it was rescued by Bank of America, the nation's largest commercial bank. Before the Bank of America purchase was announced, Merrill began to post huge losses because many of the subprime bonds it had securitized were now going bad. In early 2008 it also closed First Franklin, the subprime lender it had bought just the year before for $1.3 billion. When it came to buying First Franklin, you might say that Merrill caught a falling knife.

Once You Decide to Jump In . . .

As mentioned previously, under the $700 billion bailout bill (EESA) the government has the power to invest in banks. In mid–October it did just that. The nine banks or investment banks (Wall Street firms) that agreed to let the government buy stakes in them were:

- Bank of America
- Bank of New York Mellon
- Citigroup
- Goldman Sachs
- JPMorgan Chase
- Merrill Lynch (which soon will be owned by Bank of America)
- Morgan Stanley
- State Street Bank
- Wells Fargo

Seven of these nine banks didn't want the government's investment, which came in the form of preferred, nonvoting shares. But no one was telling Treasury secretary Henry Paulson what to do during this time. (Note that Uncle Sam was investing in Mr. Paulson's former company, Goldman Sachs, among others.)

There will be more government investments in banks and S&Ls, so stay tuned. But does this mean you too should invest in these publicly traded depositories? You might look at Uncle Sam's investment in these banks and figure the government will in no way let them fail. That's probably true, and as we noted, most of these banks didn't need Uncle Sam's money. It was a psychological move by Paulson to show the world that our banks are still strong—and if you didn't believe him he's going to invest even more money in them just to doubly prove his point.

So, should you invest in banks?

Answer: Only if you have money to burn should you speculate on bank stocks, though there is language in the bill that says if the government invests in a bank by taking stock warrants, the bank must protect the Treasury against stock dilution.

Translation: If the government invests in a bank, that bank cannot go out and issue more shares, because such a move might potentially hurt the Treasury's position. Even so, until the financial smoke clears tread lightly.

So-called sin or vice stocks are sometimes recommended as a safe haven during tough times. This would include companies that are involved in the manufacture of such things as alcohol, tobacco, and entertainment (movies, video games, DVDs). Some equities analysts throw casinos into this category as well, but given where unemployment is headed in this country I'm doubtful fun seekers will be visiting the blackjack table as frequently as they were earlier in the decade, especially if they need to gas up the SUV. When times are tough, people drink more—which means they purchase increased quantities of booze. If you want to profit from the expected increase in narcotized drunks roaming the streets crying about their lost investment in Bear Stearns, Fannie Mae, or Freddie Mac and you can still sleep at night, that's up to you; but I'll see you at confession on Saturday afternoon.

And finally, there are entertainment companies to consider as an investment. During the Great Depression the movie business in this country thrived. Back then matinees cost five cents and you got to see two shows. This time around it's $9.

Safe Havens: Ginnie Mae and Treasury Bond Mutual Funds

The Government National Mortgage Association (GNMA, Ginnie Mae) puts its guarantee on mortgage bonds where insurance is provided to homeowners who take out a loan to buy a house. The insurance comes from two government sources: the Federal Housing

Administration (FHA), which is part of the Department of Housing and Urban Development (HUD), and the Department of Veterans Affairs (VA). The FHA accounts for the lion's share of the insurance that is written each year.

Investors buy GNMA securities and Uncle Sam (who gets his money from us, the taxpayers) guarantees the payments no matter what. First, a little back story: In the 1980s, FHA/VA-insured loans accounted for 10 percent to 15 percent of all new mortgages originated in the United States. When the subprime industry boomed from 2002 to 2007, FHA/VA-insured loans accounted for fewer than 3 in 100 loans originated, or less than 3 percent. And for years GNMA was jokingly nicknamed by mortgage professionals as the "government's subprime program" because it catered to home buyers who could not get a mortgage in the private sector—that is, until Wall Street firms like Merrill Lynch began financing subprime lenders that were hungry to make a loan to anyone with a pulse.

Subprime mortgages originated by private-sector firms like First Franklin (Merrill Lynch, that is) carry delinquency rates north of 30 percent. Meanwhile, the "government's subprime program" is doing just fine. One Vanguard GNMA mutual fund I invested in (symbol: VFIIX) returned 2.49 percent through early October of 2008. The underlying FHA and VA loans backing these bonds have late payments as high as 14 percent, but the fund managed to return 2.49 percent. How can that be? Answer: The government insures the yield on the underlying GNMA securities. It may be socialism, but it works for me.

Whether you're investing 401(k) money or a regular account, one of the safest places to park your money is U.S. Treasury notes and bonds. As long as the U.S. government doesn't go bankrupt, Treasuries are one of the safest havens out there. You won't make a ton of money, but you'll preserve your principal—and make a little. Hey, it beats losing 30 percent in the stock market. In 2008, mutual funds that offered long-term Treasuries had returns just shy of 4 percent.

A Word about Gold

You've heard it before and you'll hear it again: In times of uncertainty—and inflation—gold is the place to be. Back in 2001, the "ancient metal of kings" was selling for just over $300 an ounce. In October 2008, the price was a nifty $900 an ounce—thanks, in part, to the disintegrating stock market. After a seven-year run-up during which its value tripled, is gold ready to top out, too? It's hard to say. To some, gold's bull might still look young because global demand for the product—jewelry manufacturers, for instance—has outstripped supply. But now that the world economy is hurting (thanks to the United States' mortgage crisis), demand could fall, sending gold down again.

The Safest Haven of All: CDs and Savings Accounts in Federally Insured Banks, S&Ls, and Credit Unions

One fear shared by consumers, business leaders, and politicians is that the credit and mortgage crisis could lead to a depression, something this country hasn't faced since the 1930s. But there's one reason why this crisis—which has spiraled into other sectors of the economy outside of housing and mortgages and then overseas—may not lead to a second Great Depression: deposit insurance. The Great Depression was ushered in by not only the stock market crash of 1929 but also bank runs. In the Roaring Twenties, banks did not have deposit insurance, which meant their customers' life savings could be wiped out if the institution failed, which was exactly what happened. From 1928 to 1932, 1,700 savings institutions failed and depositors lost $200 million—a phenomenal amount of money back then.

Now may not be the time to invest in the stocks of publicly traded banks and S&Ls, but one thing is certain: savings accounts and certificates of deposit (CDs) are insured by the federal government through the Federal Deposit Insurance Corporation (FDIC). Prior to passage of the Emergency Economic Stabilization Act (EESA), the maximum government insurance on a savings, CD, or checking account was $100,000. The EESA bill raised the limit to $250,000 per account. A few weeks later the FDIC and Treasury issued more clarifications that basically said every single deposit is insured no matter the size. This means all your money in the bank—no matter how much you have there—is protected in the case the institution fails. Millionaires can now sleep easy at night.

During the height of the stock market meltdown in October, I remember seeing a handful of advertisements in the local paper from financial institutions offering certificates of deposit at attractive yields, some north of 4 percent (though you had to lock up your money for five years). You may not get rich from your CDs, but this isn't about getting rich. It's about capital preservation. Cash is king.

Chapter 4

Taxes and Politics

EESA Digs a Deeper Money Hole for All of Us

"I have debts that no honest man can pay."
—Bruce Springsteen, from the song "Atlantic City"

When the House of Representatives first took up the Emergency Economic Stabilization Act (EESA) in September 2008, it was a clean bill: one where the intended legislative mission was laid out in plain language, with no extras. Even though EESA was written in such general terms (leaving it open to interpretation), it stuck to the mission of allowing the government to buy troubled mortgage assets from banks (and cities, foreign governments, and so on) and to purchase ownership stakes in those banks. It set up the Troubled Asset Relief Program (TARP) and how it would presumably work, and laid out provisions where members of Congress and the public could review the Treasury Department's actions and sales.

But then the media and tabloid coverage exploded, and the cries of "No bailout for millionaires on Wall Street" intensified. Many Republican members of Congress, already behind in tough reelection bids, voted no. President Bush, whose popularity with the American public was reaching new lows every day (because of the economy, oil prices, and the war), was pushing hard for the bill, but the GOP rank and file were trying to unlink from the president. House minority leader John Boehner of Ohio thought he had enough yes votes among his fellow Republicans. On Monday, September 29, 2008, the vote came late in the morning—broadcast live on both C-SPAN and the business channel CNBC. On the New York Stock Exchange (NYSE), traders watched nervously, sweating, their eyes focused on various TV screens. At first it looked as though the bill would pass, but then the vote count changed and quickly the "sell" orders began to tumble in, creating a new crash on Wall Street.

Two-thirds of House Republicans shot it down. With the election just around the corner and surveys pointing toward a possible landslide by the Democrats, GOP members of Congress were listening to the phone calls and reading the thousands of e-mails from their constituents. The message was clear: "Don't you dare bail out them rascals on Wall Street—they caused this mortgage and credit crisis mess" was the rallying cry heard on talk radio and some of the wild hairs who called in to C-SPAN. The final tally on the vote was 228 against and 205 in favor. About two-thirds of Democrats voted for it.

Shortly after the vote, Boehner of Ohio, dressed in a dark suit and pink tie, was surrounded by reporters in the Capitol building. Shoving microphones in his face, the press asked what had gone wrong. "I have some members who would do anything for me, and I talked to them. It killed me, absolutely killed me when they told me they couldn't vote yes."

By day's end, the Dow had fallen 778 points. The selling was so intense that only 162 stocks rose on the NYSE while 3,073 fell. If Americans—Republicans and Democrats alike—were angry before because $700 billion of their tax dollars (not yet approved) would be used "to bail out Wall Street" (as the slogans said), then they suddenly had another reason to hate their elected officials: Dude, you shrunk my 401(k). At work and at home millions of Americans who dared to look saw that on paper their retirement plans and other savings had evaporated.

The Republicans who voted against the bill had some explaining to do. They cited all the phone calls and e-mails from their constituents urging them to vote no. Some also blamed House Speaker Nancy Pelosi of California for making what they called a "partisan speech" before the vote on the House floor. In her remarks the Speaker, among other things, blamed the Bush White House for the lack of financial regulation that had occurred over the past eight years. But as the political newspaper *Politico* pointed out, the speech made by the California Democrat "suffered more from its rambling sentences than political jabs, and it was a reminder to most how exhausted both sides had become after long negotiations leading up" to the vote on the $700 billion bailout.

But what were the House of Represntatives and the Senate to do now? The stock market had been decimated. (It recovered a few hundred points the next day, Tuesday, but then kept plunging.) The Jewish holiday Rosh Hashanah started at sundown, and some elected officials—including Representative Barney Frank, Democrat of Massachusetts and a key player in drafting the bill (Frank was chairman of the House Banking Committee)—were taking the next two days off. The Senate moved forward, promising to get something done. Treasury secretary Henry Paulson, the man pushing harder than anyone else for the $700 billion, was constantly reminding the White House to use its influence (as much as it could) to sway more GOP members of Congress to change their vote to "yea" from "nay."

On Wednesday, the Senate voted on its version of the bill, which passed by a huge margin, 74 to 25. The Senate version, you might say, was a little fatter than the House bill: 451 pages to about 110. The House bill was sleek and trim and addressed only the credit and mortgage market mess the nation faced. The Senate legislation did that, too, but its extra 341 pages included a slew of tax provisions.

Many of these tax provisions were not new; rather, they were extensions or expansions of former tax breaks that either had expired or were set to expire this year. So, it seems plausible that these provisions were added to the bill in order to sway those original "nay" voters by furthering their existing tax agendas. In other words, it seems that they were tacked on by legislators for expediency and convenience. Would all the extra tax breaks have been approved eventually? Probably. It's just a matter of when and in what form of legislation.

On Friday, the House passed the Senate bill, all 451 pages of it. Less than two hours later Bush signed the monster. After he did, the Washington watchdog group, Taxpayers for Common Sense, spent the weekend adding up how much all these extra tax provisions might cost the U.S. Treasury over time. Its estimate came to $110 billion—which means the cost of the bailout bill could actually turn out to be $810 billion (the $700 billion plus the $110 billion).

What Tax "Bennies" Were Actually Given Away?

The tax breaks signed into law by President Bush are mostly extensions of existing tax credits and exclusions of some manufacturers from taxes. A tax credit means a business does not have to pay revenue it might normally owe to the Treasury. Less revenue means a larger budget deficit for the United States, but we will discuss that a bit later.

The passage of the so-called extender bill is an annual ritual performed by Congress. As is the case every year, the 2008 extender bill was delayed due to a dispute between Republicans and Democrats over its cost. But TARP gave Congress a perfect cover to push the bill through. Though these provisions have nothing at all to do with the mortgage and credit crisis, in Washington you have to give something to get something.

Following is a list of many of the tax breaks and extensions that were added to the EESA bill to lobby members of Congress and senators to vote yes:

- Wind and refined coal facilities (the latter could be liquid or gaseous fuel made from coal).
- Biomass facilities (plant matter grown to generate electricity).
- Nonhydroelectric dams.
- Energy companies that derive power from marine (ocean/lake) and hydrokinetic sources.
- Public power companies that issue bonds to build clean, renewable energy facilities.
- Companies that make fuel out of what's called "coal waste sludge."
- Firms disposing of carbon dioxide.
- Manufacturers of biodiesel and renewable diesel fuel, some of which is used for aviation fuel. The credit doesn't apply if a U.S. manufacturer produces it outside the United States.
- Businesses owning plug-in electric vehicles weighing between 10,000 pounds and 26,000 pounds. The tax credit can vary between $7,500 and $15,000 per truck.
- Manufacturers of "idling reduction units" and "advanced insulation" used in trucks. These firms are excluded from the government's tax on heavy trucks.
- Energy conservation bonds, including some bonds issued by Indian tribal governments.
- Owners of commercial buildings that are deemed energy efficient (for instance, if they grow grass on the roof).
- Restaurant owners who make physical improvements to their retail spaces.
- Importers of rum made in Puerto Rico and the Virgin Islands.
- Manufacturers of wooden arrows, but only if they are "designed for use by children." (A lobbyist somewhere is smiling over this one.)
- Mine rescue teams.

- Business properties on Indian reservations (a business property, presumably, is a for-profit enterprise).
- Motor sports racetrack facilities (NASCAR and others; this could cost the government $100 million over time).
- Film and television production companies (a tax incentive that makes it more lucrative for media firms to shoot movies and TV programs in the United States).
- Wool product manufacturers (they must be based in the United States but can import yarns and other materials from overseas).

The bill has many other vague benefits for businesses, such as extension of tax credits for companies conducting research and experiments in the United States. According to the group Taxpayers for Common Sense, giants of commerce benefit mostly from this clause—Boeing, Electronic Data Systems, Harley-Davidson, Microsoft, and others. The group says this tax break alone could cost the Treasury (taxpayers) $19 billion over two years. What do research tax credits have to do with the mortgage and credit crisis? Answer: nothing. American Samoa also benefits because EESA extends tax credits for economic development on that Pacific island.

But the consumer isn't totally left out. Americans can receive an extension on tax credits for owning:

- Solar energy property.
- Fuel cell power.
- "Small wind energy" (talk to the company that sold you the mini-windmill in your backyard).
- Geothermal heat pumps.
- Residential energy-efficient properties, including solar.
- Plug-in electric cars (a tax credit of up to $2,500).
- Bicycle commuters. (This is an extension of tax breaks tied to employers who give reimbursements to employees who commute to work on their bikes. The reimbursements can cover the purchase of a bike, repair, and improvements.)

- Stoves that use biomass matter (plant derived mostly).
- Energy-efficient dishwashers, clothes washers, and refrigerators (manufactured in 2008 or after).
- "Smart meters" used to run furnaces and other home heating devices.

Oh, and there are tax benefits for people who work in hazardous jobs. For instance, if you receive money from the Black Lung Disability Trust Fund, you're in luck—you'll be getting more money, too. (If you receive this benefit, chances are you were a coal miner.) If you happen to be a plaintiff in the *Exxon Valdez* oil spill case, you can now average out the cash award you receive in the case over three years instead of suffering a one-time tax hit.

Besides the tax giveaways listed here, there are many others that are so obtusely worded that it is unclear what is being given away and how a normal middle-class citizen is affected. Some have to do with investing money in stocks, securities, and the treatment of dividends.

Also, there are tax deductions for "certain expenses" of elementary and secondary school teachers. There is one plus for all Americans with health care plans: Their insurance providers must now extend coverage for mental health and substance abuse, treating these like other diseases. (Check with your human resources department at work for details.)

The government also extended tax relief for middle-class filers affected by the alternative minimum tax (AMT). Originally, the AMT was created to make sure rich folks didn't get away with not paying enough in tax. Over time, more and more middle-class citizens are becoming ensnared in the program, causing them to owe significantly more in taxes. This is due to the failure of the original AMT law to account for inflation. In the EESA bill the exemption from the AMT is raised to $69,950 and $46,200 for joint and single filers, respectively, from $66,250 and $44,350.

Certain tax breaks also are extended to people who have suffered through the 2008 Midwestern storms, floods, and tornadoes, as well as those affected by the hurricanes in the Gulf of Mexico. And last, there is a tax incentive for investing in the city of Washington itself, where most members of Congress spend five days a week when in session.

The strange thing about all the tax giveaways is that none really have anything to do with home ownership, housing, and mortgages, which might leave some of us scratching our heads. To get the bill passed, much was given away. That leaves us with some key questions.

Do I, as an individual filer, get any kind of tax break on my mortgage, especially if I'm current on my payments?

Answer: No. But if you invest in any of the companies that receive tax breaks, you could benefit. Plus, you might be eligible for some of the consumer provisions I've outlined.

What about the mortgage "cram down" provision of the bill where homeowners filing for bankruptcy protection can ask a judge to reduce, or cram down, the size of their mortgage, saving them money?

Answer: Some of that language was in early versions of the bill. Some Democrats were for it because they felt it helped lower- and middle-class Americans who might have been sold mortgages they could not afford. (The cram down provision also would have helped wealthier Americans in bankruptcy who owned homes.) But the language giving a judge such power was defeated, thanks to lobbying efforts by the Mortgage Bankers Association and banking trade groups. Moral of story: Don't ever underestimate the power of lobbyists working for the financial services industry.

So, as an individual, what do I get?

Answer: There are a few things for individuals to be happy about in this bill. The AMT relief just outlined is very important, as being ensnared in the AMT can be very costly. There are other things to look out for as well. First, the bill allows you to deduct state and local sales taxes rather than state and local income taxes. This benefits people living in no-income-tax states, or those in low-income-tax states who purchased a major item in the year, like a car. The bill also allows taxpayers to deduct up to $4,000 of qualified higher education tuition and fees "above the line," which translated means that this reduces your actual taxable income. (There are income restrictions.) Finally, the bill extends through 2012 a provision that generally allows homeowners to avoid paying federal income tax on debt forgiveness received in connection with a foreclosure or a mortgage workout on a principal residence.

AN UGLY FACT

Among other things, the EESA bill raises the nation's debt ceiling to $11.3 trillion. In the fall of 2008, right after the bill was signed into law by President Bush, the U.S. government owed $10.3 trillion—money that was financed through the sale of U.S. Treasury bonds. In the current fiscal year, the government will spend more than $500 billion just to pay interest on those massive borrowings. The money, of course, comes from the nation's taxpayers.

What Do All These Tax Breaks Mean for the Consumer?

Most of the revenue brought into the government comes from federal income tax payments that are paid by individuals and companies. When the government spends more than it takes in, that results in a budget deficit. The U.S. government has been running annual budget deficits for years, except for a few times during the Clinton years when we somehow managed to run a surplus. With the U.S. economy in a recession, that means more people are unemployed. Higher unemployment results in less federal income tax paid, which in turn means less revenue. Less revenue will mean higher annual budget deficits—unless the government can cut spending, which it never seems to do.

KEY ISSUE

For the fiscal year that ends in the fall of 2009, the forecast is for a federal budget deficit of $1 trillion, thanks in part to the $700 billion used for EESA and all those tax breaks for businesses and consumers. For the fiscal year that ended on September 30, 2008, the deficit was $455 billion; the year before, it was $162 billion.

So at what point will the U.S. government go bankrupt?

No matter how you slice it, $1 trillion is a lot of money and $10.3 trillion is *a whole lot* of money. After a while, the debt numbers on what we as a nation owe become so large it's like trying to comprehend outer space. The universe and our government's debt have one thing in common: Both seem to go on forever. As I pointed out earlier, in the new paradigm of American finance, one where our financial institutions are now partly owned by the government, there is a new definition for liquidity, and it goes like this: Any company (bank, investment bank, etc.) or government is liquid (solvent) as long as investors are willing to lend it money. As long as our investors (China, Japan, and U.S. banks and corporations) keep buying our government securities, we can stay in business. If not, we'll have to raise the interest rate we pay to get investors to buy our Treasury securities. This will effectively raise interest for all sorts of loans, including mortgages. If we pay higher rates of return (higher interest rates) and investors still do not buy our

Treasury securities, then the ball game is over. We all go home (if we still have a home) and break up furniture to burn in our fireplaces.

The bottom line is that there are two ways to balance a budget—whether it's a government budget, a household budget, or a business budget: bring more revenue in or cut spending. It's as simple as that. The political debate over taxes has been raging in this nation for more than two decades. Most Americans do not want their taxes raised. States are forced to raise taxes because, unlike the federal government, they cannot, by law, spend more than they take in. The Feds can put off tax increases forever by continuing to borrow by selling Treasury bonds. Tax breaks to businesses and consumers mean less money goes into the federal budget—which means bigger deficits if spending isn't decreased. As a nation of citizens balancing the U.S. budget, it boils down to this: Do you want to receive less in services or do want to owe less in taxes? The only way the government can cut spending is to trim its massive budgets. The three largest budget items for Uncle Sam are the Treasury (which spends $525 billion annually to pay interest on all the bonds we've already sold); the Department of Defense (which spends $630 billion to build weapons and protect our nation); and the Department of Health and Human Services (which accounts for just over $700 billion on various medical insurance programs to cover the uninsured and our senior citizens). Every other government agency spends $100 billion or less.

The more money we spend to bail out our banks, the less money we have to spend on other government programs—whether they are health insurance, housing, or education. If you want something, you have to pay for it. And that means taxes.

The Last Word: Politics

When the $700 billion bailout became big news in early September, the battle cry heard on talk radio was "No bailout for Wall Street millionaires." The lefties at ACORN were against it, as were the angry fans of talk radio. Finally, our citizens had found a common enemy: those dirtbag Wall Street chieftains and bankers who had caused the mortgage and credit crisis.

While the bailout was being negotiated, our elected officials who were left of center saw this as a chance to crack down on some of the excessive pay packages our barons of finance have been earning. (Angelo Mozilo of Countrywide Home Loans, once the nation's largest subprime lender, made $400 million by selling his stock in the company over the past three years.) Those who were the friends of big business (including Wall Street and banking) continued to be laissez-faire in their approach, resisting any government controls on how much an executive can earn.

Under EESA, no price caps were legislated on how much money a businessperson can earn—unless the company participates in the Troubled Asset Relief Program (TARP). Caps under TARP include:

- Limit the tax write-offs for executive compensation above $500,000 for companies that sell distressed assets to the government.
- Prohibit golden parachute payments to executives whose companies are selling troubled assets directly to the government under the TARP program. (A golden parachute means that a departing company executive—forced out or otherwise—is entitled to a lot of money.) If the government purchases from a firm, via auction, $300 million or more in troubled assets, similar limits on bonuses and other executive compensation might apply.

It's too early to say exactly what the political fallout will be from TARP. Some members of Congress and senators might eventually lose their jobs because they voted for it. But they also have a good excuse for pulling the "yea" lever: The stock market was in a free fall. What were they supposed to do?

Traditionally, Republicans have been seen as friends of big business and Wall Street, whereas Democrats have been friends of the

KEY ISSUE

None of the banks participating in the nationalization portion of TARP, the one where the Treasury Department bought stakes in the nine largest banks, seem to be too concerned about the payment limits. Shortly before the bill was passed, Neel Kashkari, the man running the TARP program for Treasury (a former Goldman Sachs banker), held a conference call explaining the golden parachute clause to bankers. (A copy of the call is available on YouTube.) He told the bankers that the pay caps in the bill are "quite reasonable" and a "pretty modest hindrance to you."

rank-and-file worker with the lunch pail. These are broad generalities, of course. Politics is more complicated than economics, involving such nonmonetary issues as the wars in Iraq and Afghanistan, abortion, gun rights, gay rights, and health care. Republicans, to their credit, can argue that for a decade they tried to crack down on Fannie Mae and Freddie Mac—that these two Congressionally chartered mortgage investing giants had grown too large and that no one really knew their true financial condition. The GOP was right on that score, but Fannie and Freddie, as I mentioned earlier, did not start the subprime crisis. It should be noted that over the past 15 years Democrats and Republicans alike received large campaign donations from executives who worked at Fannie and Freddie—and also received money from their political action committees (PACs). It might be argued that in exchange for the donations, members of Congress and senators shot down efforts to place tighter controls on them—call it "legal bribery." (When the government seized control of Fannie and Freddie in September, one of the first things their chief regulator, James Lockhart, did was order an immediate halt to all lobbying activities.)

Fannie and Freddie did not invent the subprime loan; they did not provide money to subprime lenders and securitize their bonds, selling them to corporations and municipalities here and then overseas. Wall Street did it. It was the money man at the top, financing subprime lenders, buying their loans for securitization, and not caring too much about the quality of what they were putting into bonds. They believed in the tooth fairy: that home prices would keep rising 20 percent a year.

It didn't turn out that way. What we have now is a financial system that has been partly socialized. The government owns Fannie, Freddie, the nation's largest insurer (American International Group), and $125 billion in preferred stock in our nine largest banks—Bank of America, Citigroup, JPMorgan Chase, and Wells Fargo among them. Soon the government will own stakes in many more banks and thrifts, and maybe some more insurance companies, too. It all happened under a Republican White House that believed in getting regulators off the backs of big business, Wall Street. Now, the White House doesn't have to worry about government being too tough on the Street. The government *is* the Street.

Epilogue

The Last Word: If I Ran the Regulatory Zoo

R egulation—we can't live with it and we can't live without it. Most of the men and women who run U.S. companies (no matter the size of that business) have probably complained somewhere along the line about too much regulation. Regulation means rules, following state and federal laws, and filling out paperwork. No one likes paperwork. It costs money, including money spent to hire accountants and lawyers who are needed to make sure those "rules and regs" are not broken.

But when you consider the fact that the American taxpayers are dishing out $700 billion (with possibly more to come) to fix the mess, something must be done to make sure such a crisis does not happen again. During the Bush years, government regulation of the Wall Street and mortgage market was lacking. Let's just say the bailout plan works—or the government gets back half the money. But what about preventing this mess from ever happening again? How do we do that? Here are a few thoughts.

- **Bring back the Glass–Steagall Act.** It was ripped down and destroyed during the final days of the Clinton administration. Glass–Steagall prevented banks from owning securities firms and securities firms from owning depositories. Passed in November 1999 and signed by President Clinton, the Gramm-Leach-Bliley Act (GLB) obliterated 66 years of safety and soundness. The odd thing about GLB is that neither banks nor Wall Street firms were hurting financially. They needed more powers like the world needed more seawater. Still, GLB was heralded by Republicans and Democrats (who didn't want to come across as antibusiness) alike. The Dems just bowed and stood aside. Think for a moment about the losses Citigroup could have avoided if it had not been allowed to underwrite subprime asset-backed securities. Yes, I know that there are few traditional Wall Street firms left. But Wall Street firms are like starfish: In time they'll regenerate. Give banks 10 years to divest themselves of their investment banking arms (securities underwriting) and cap their ownership in securities firms at 10 percent. No exceptions.

- **Regulate Wall Street and the credit default swap (CDS) market.** A former loan trader at Nomura once explained to me how credit default swaps magnified the mortgage crisis. This trader, requesting his name not be used, noted that in 2005 and 2006 $40 billion worth of BBB-rated subprime bonds came to market. These were the subordinated pieces of larger securitizations—the ones that took the first losses when the market crashed. He noted that in the scheme of things $40 billion might not seem like a huge number. But the dollar volume of credit default swaps written against that $40 billion totaled $130 billion. This means that insurers (a swap is essentially an insurance contract) might have to shell out $130 billion of coverage if all those BBB pieces go bad. American International Group (AIG), alone, had exposure on $70 billion worth of subprime CDSs. In other words, more bets were taken against a game than the total size of the game. Crazy stuff.

    Here's the kicker: Not one federal regulatory agency—not the Securities and Exchange Commission (SEC), not the Commodity Futures Trading Commission (CFTC)—regulates the CDS market in any meaningful way. How do we know an insurer can cover the bets it made? Answer: We don't. In other words, a credit default swap is a way to gamble. But at least the casinos in Las Vegas have to answer to the State Gaming Control Board. Credit default swaps players have no one—and there are roughly $44 trillion worth of these bets out there, some of which will pay off. This means whichever firm wrote the policy (AIG and others) has to pay up. This is potentially a black hole for the entire U.S. economy.

- **Require all individual retail mortgage loan officers, loan brokers, and wholesale account executives to be licensed and state certified.** Anyone facilitating a loan must pass a test—and cannot use the license of a company. I'm talking about individuals, not firms. (Under current law, mortgage banking firms must receive state approvals before they can fund mortgages.) Yes, I know any type of certification requirement will cost money, but too bad. After blowing a $1 trillion hole in the U.S. economy, having licensed loan officers (LOs), account executives (AEs), and brokers is a small price to pay. Professionals may not want to shell out the money to get certified, but at the very least it will distinguish the professionals from the fast-buck artists.

- **Regulate hedge funds.** What is a hedge fund? Answer: a group of men and women who manage (invest) money for rich individuals, corporations, municipalities, and so on. Does each and every hedge fund have to register with the SEC? Answer: not that I know of. If hedge funds are buying and selling publicly traded securities (stocks and bonds), then they should register with the SEC. Each quarter, hedge funds should be forced to disclose their positions (long and short) if they own more than 1 percent of a company. If they don't like it, too bad. All the cash that hedge funds manage can be used to resurrect Wall Street—but this time with regulation.

Feel free to show these ideas to your members of Congress and senators in Washington. If they don't like these suggestions, then you ask them how much money they've been receiving (in the form of campaign donations) from investment bankers.

Excerpts from the Emergency Economic Stabilization Act of 2008

I n most cases, members of Congress don't actually write legislation themselves. (This probably comes as no shock to Americans.) Often the language is drafted by staffers or even lobbyists who nine times out of ten have a law degree, which means for the layman the reading can be turgid. What follows is a selection of excerpts from the 451-page bill passed by the U.S. Senate, then the House of Representatives, and then ultimately signed into law by President Bush in early October. We have included portions of the "financial" section of the bill that deals with the Troubled Asset Relief Program (TARP), whose initial goal was to buy mortgages and other assets from financial institutions—and to invest government money in those institutions. Also included in this section are excerpt portions of the tax provisions granted to businesses and consumers. Happy reading.

AMENDMENT NO. _____   Calendar No. _____

Purpose: In the nature of a substitute.

IN THE SENATE OF THE UNITED STATES—110th Cong., 2d Sess.

H. R. 1424

To amend section 712 of the Employee Retirement Income Security Act of 1974, section 2705 of the Public Health Service Act, section 9812 of the Internal Revenue Code of 1986 to require equity in the provision of mental health and substance-related disorder benefits under group health plans, to prohibit discrimination on the basis of genetic information with respect to health insurance and employment, and for other purposes.

Referred to the Committee on _____ and
ordered to be printed

Ordered to lie on the table and to be printed

AMENDMENT IN THE NATURE OF A SUBSTITUTE intended
to be proposed by _____

Viz:
Strike all after the enacting clause and insert the following:

DIVISION A—EMERGENCY ECONOMIC STABILIZATION

SECTION 1. SHORT TITLE AND TABLE OF CONTENTS.

(a) SHORT TITLE.—This division may be cited as the "Emergency Economic Stabilization Act of 2008".

(b) TABLE OF CONTENTS.—The table of contents for this division is as follows:

Sec. 1. Short title and table of contents.
Sec. 2. Purposes.
Sec. 3. Definitions.

TITLE I—TROUBLED ASSETS RELIEF PROGRAM

Sec. 101. Purchases of troubled assets.
Sec. 102. Insurance of troubled assets.
Sec. 103. Considerations.
Sec. 104. Financial Stability Oversight Board.
Sec. 105. Reports.
Sec. 106. Rights; management; sale of troubled assets; revenues and sale proceeds.
Sec. 107. Contracting procedures.
Sec. 108. Conflicts of interest.
Sec. 109. Foreclosure mitigation efforts.
Sec. 110. Assistance to homeowners.
Sec. 111. Executive compensation and corporate governance.
Sec. 112. Coordination with foreign authorities and central banks.
Sec. 113. Minimization of long-term costs and maximization of benefits for taxpayers.
Sec. 114. Market transparency.
Sec. 115. Graduated authorization to purchase.
Sec. 116. Oversight and audits.
Sec. 117. Study and report on margin authority.
Sec. 118. Funding.
Sec. 119. Judicial review and related matters.
Sec. 120. Termination of authority.
Sec. 121. Special Inspector General for the Troubled Asset Relief Program.
Sec. 122. Increase in statutory limit on the public debt.
Sec. 123. Credit reform.
Sec. 124. HOPE for Homeowners amendments.
Sec. 125. Congressional Oversight Panel.
Sec. 126. FDIC authority.
Sec. 127. Cooperation with the FBI.
Sec. 128. Acceleration of effective date.
Sec. 129. Disclosures on exercise of loan authority.
Sec. 130. Technical corrections.
Sec. 131. Exchange Stabilization Fund reimbursement.
Sec. 132. Authority to suspend mark-to-market accounting.
Sec. 133. Study on mark-to-market accounting.
Sec. 134. Recoupment.
Sec. 135. Preservation of authority.
Sec. 136. Temporary increase in deposit and share insurance coverage.

TITLE II—BUDGET-RELATED PROVISIONS

Sec. 201. Information for congressional support agencies.
Sec. 202. Reports by the Office of Management and Budget and the Congressional Budget Office.
Sec. 203. Analysis in President's Budget.
Sec. 204. Emergency treatment.

TITLE III—TAX PROVISIONS

Sec. 301. Gain or loss from sale or exchange of certain preferred stock.
Sec. 302. Special rules for tax treatment of executive compensation of employers participating in the troubled assets relief program.
Sec. 303. Extension of exclusion of income from discharge of qualified principal residence indebtedness.

SEC. 2. PURPOSES.

The purposes of this Act are—

(1) to immediately provide authority and facilities that the Secretary of the Treasury can use to restore liquidity and stability to the financial system of the United States; and

(2) to ensure that such authority and such facilities are used in a manner that—

(A) protects home values, college funds, retirement accounts, and life savings;

(B) preserves homeownership and promotes jobs and economic growth;

(C) maximizes overall returns to the taxpayers of the United States; and

(D) provides public accountability for the exercise of such authority.

SEC. 3. DEFINITIONS.

For purposes of this Act, the following definitions shall apply:

(1) APPROPRIATE COMMITTEES OF CONGRESS.—The term "appropriate committees of Congress" means—

(A) the Committee on Banking, Housing, and Urban Affairs, the Committee on Finance, the Committee on the Budget, and the Committee on Appropriations of the Senate; and

(B) the Committee on Financial Services, the Committee on Ways and Means, the Committee on the Budget, and the Committee on Appropriations of the House of Representatives.

(2) BOARD.—The term "Board" means the Board of Governors of the Federal Reserve System.

(3) CONGRESSIONAL SUPPORT AGENCIES.—The term "congressional support agencies" means the Congressional Budget Office and the Joint Committee on Taxation.

(4) CORPORATION.—The term "Corporation" means the Federal Deposit Insurance Corporation.

(5) FINANCIAL INSTITUTION.—The term "financial institution" means any institution, including, but not limited to, any bank, savings association, credit union, security broker or dealer, or insurance company, established and regulated under the laws of the United States or any State, territory, or possession of the United States, the District of Columbia, Commonwealth of Puerto Rico, Commonwealth of Northern Mariana Islands, Guam, American Samoa, or the United States Virgin Islands, and having significant operations in the United States, but excluding any central bank of, or institution owned by, a foreign government.

(6) FUND.—The term "Fund" means the Troubled Assets Insurance Financing Fund established under section 102.

(7) SECRETARY.—The term "Secretary" means the Secretary of the Treasury.

(8) TARP.—The term "TARP" means the Troubled Asset Relief Program established under section 101.

(9) TROUBLED ASSETS.—The term "troubled assets" means—

(A) residential or commercial mortgages and any securities, obligations, or other instruments that are based on or related to such mortgages, that in each case was originated or issued on or before March 14, 2008, the purchase of which the Secretary determines promotes financial market stability; and

(B) any other financial instrument that the Secretary, after consultation with the Chairman of the Board of Governors of the Federal Reserve System, determines the purchase of which is necessary to promote financial market stability, but only upon transmittal of such determination, in writing, to the appropriate committees of Congress.

TITLE I—TROUBLED ASSETS RELIEF PROGRAM

SEC. 101. PURCHASES OF TROUBLED ASSETS.

(a) OFFICES; AUTHORITY.—

(1) AUTHORITY.—The Secretary is authorized to establish the Troubled Asset Relief Program (or "TARP") to purchase, and to make and fund commitments to purchase, troubled assets from any financial institution, on such terms and conditions as are determined by the Secretary, and in accordance with this Act and the policies and procedures developed and published by the Secretary.

(2) COMMENCEMENT OF PROGRAM.—Establishment of the policies and procedures and other similar administrative requirements imposed on the Secretary by this Act are not intended to delay the commencement of the TARP.

(3) ESTABLISHMENT OF TREASURY OFFICE.—

(A) IN GENERAL.—The Secretary shall implement any program under paragraph (1) through an Office of Financial Stability, established for such purpose within the Office of Domestic Finance of the Department of the Treasury, which office shall be headed by an Assistant Secretary of the Treasury, appointed by the President, by and with the advice and consent of the Senate, except that an interim Assistant Secretary may be appointed by the Secretary.

    (B) CLERICAL AMENDMENTS.—

        (i) TITLE 5.—Section 5315 of title 5, United States Code, is amended in the item relating to Assistant Secretaries of the Treasury, by striking "(9)" and inserting "(10)".

        (ii) TITLE 31.—Section 301(e) of title 31, United States Code, is amended by striking "9" and inserting "10".

(b) CONSULTATION.—In exercising the authority under this section, the Secretary shall consult with the Board, the Corporation, the Comptroller of the Currency, the Director of the Office of Thrift Supervision, and the Secretary of Housing and Urban Development.

(c) NECESSARY ACTIONS.—The Secretary is authorized to take such actions as the Secretary deems necessary to carry out the authorities in this Act, including, without limitation, the following:

    (1) The Secretary shall have direct hiring authority with respect to the appointment of employees to administer this Act.

    (2) Entering into contracts, including contracts for services authorized by section 3109 of title 5, United States Code.

    (3) Designating financial institutions as financial agents of the Federal Government, and such institutions shall perform all such reasonable duties related to this Act as financial agents of the Federal Government as may be required.

    (4) In order to provide the Secretary with the flexibility to manage troubled assets in a manner designed to minimize cost to the taxpayers, establishing vehicles that are authorized, subject to supervision by the Secretary, to purchase, hold, and sell troubled assets and issue obligations.

    (5) Issuing such regulations and other guidance as may be necessary or appropriate to define terms or carry out the authorities or purposes of this Act.

(d) PROGRAM GUIDELINES.—Before the earlier of the end of the 2-business-day period beginning on the date of the first purchase of troubled assets pursuant to the authority under this section or the end of the 45-day period beginning on the date of enactment of this Act, the Secretary shall publish program guidelines, including the following:

    (1) Mechanisms for purchasing troubled assets.

    (2) Methods for pricing and valuing troubled assets.

    (3) Procedures for selecting asset managers.

    (4) Criteria for identifying troubled assets for purchase.

(e) PREVENTING UNJUST ENRICHMENT.—In making purchases under the authority of this Act, the Secretary shall take such steps as may be necessary to prevent unjust enrichment of financial institutions participating in a program established under this section, including by preventing the sale of a troubled asset to the Secretary at a higher price than what the seller paid to purchase the asset. This subsection does not apply to troubled assets acquired in a merger or acquisition, or a purchase of assets from a financial institution in conservatorship or receivership, or that has initiated bankruptcy proceedings under title 11, United States Code.

SEC. 102. INSURANCE OF TROUBLED ASSETS.

(a) AUTHORITY.—

(1) IN GENERAL.—If the Secretary establishes the program authorized under section 101, then the Secretary shall establish a program to guarantee troubled assets originated or issued prior to March 14, 2008, including mortgage-backed securities.

(2) GUARANTEES.—In establishing any program under this subsection, the Secretary may develop guarantees of troubled assets and the associated premiums for such guarantees. Such guarantees and premiums may be determined by category or class of the troubled assets to be guaranteed.

(3) EXTENT OF GUARANTEE.—Upon request of a financial institution, the Secretary may guarantee the timely payment of principal of, and interest on, troubled assets in amounts not to exceed 100 percent of such payments. Such guarantee may be on such terms and conditions as are determined by the Secretary, provided that such terms and conditions are consistent with the purposes of this Act.

(b) REPORTS.—Not later than 90 days after the date of enactment of this Act, the Secretary shall report to the appropriate committees of Congress on the program established under subsection (a).

(c) PREMIUMS.—

(1) IN GENERAL.—The Secretary shall collect premiums from any financial institution participating in the program established under subsection (a). Such premiums shall be in an amount that the Secretary determines necessary to meet the purposes of this Act and to provide sufficient reserves pursuant to paragraph (3).

(2) AUTHORITY TO BASE PREMIUMS ON PRODUCT RISK.—In establishing any premium under paragraph (1), the Secretary may provide for variations in such rates according to the credit risk associated with the particular troubled asset that is being guaranteed. The Secretary shall publish the methodology for setting the premium for a class of troubled assets together with an explanation of the appropriateness of the class of assets for participation in the program established under this section. The methodology shall ensure that the premium is consistent with paragraph (3).

(3) MINIMUM LEVEL.—The premiums referred to in paragraph (1) shall be set by the Secretary at a level necessary to create reserves sufficient to meet anticipated claims, based on an actuarial analysis, and to ensure that taxpayers are fully protected.

(4) ADJUSTMENT TO PURCHASE AUTHORITY.— The purchase authority limit in section 115 shall be reduced by an amount equal to the difference between the total of the outstanding guaranteed obligations and the balance in the Troubled Assets Insurance Financing Fund.

(d) TROUBLED ASSETS INSURANCE FINANCING FUND.—

(1) DEPOSITS.—The Secretary shall deposit fees collected under this section into the Fund established under paragraph (2).

(2) ESTABLISHMENT.—There is established a Troubled Assets Insurance Financing Fund that shall consist of the amounts collected pursuant to paragraph (1), and any balance in such fund shall be invested by the Secretary in United States Treasury securities, or kept in cash on hand or on deposit, as necessary.

(3) PAYMENTS FROM FUND.—The Secretary shall make payments from amounts deposited in the Fund to fulfill obligations of the guarantees provided to financial institutions under subsection (a).

SEC. 103. CONSIDERATIONS.

In exercising the authorities granted in this Act, the Secretary shall take into consideration—

(1) protecting the interests of taxpayers by maximizing overall returns and minimizing the impact on the national debt;

(2) providing stability and preventing disruption to financial markets in order to limit the impact on the economy and protect American jobs, savings, and retirement security;

(3) the need to help families keep their homes and to stabilize communities;

(4) in determining whether to engage in a direct purchase from an individual financial institution, the long-term viability of the financial institution in determining whether the purchase represents the most efficient use of funds under this Act;

(5) ensuring that all financial institutions are eligible to participate in the program, without discrimination based on size, geography, form of organization, or the size, type, and number of assets eligible for purchase under this Act;

(6) providing financial assistance to financial institutions, including those serving low- and moderate-income populations and other underserved communities, and that have assets less than $1,000,000,000, that were well or adequately capitalized as of June 30, 2008, and that as a result of the devaluation of the preferred government-sponsored enterprises stock will drop one or more

capital levels, in a manner sufficient to restore the financial institutions to at least an adequately capitalized level;

(7) the need to ensure stability for United States public instrumentalities, such as counties and cities, that may have suffered significant increased costs or losses in the current market turmoil;

(8) protecting the retirement security of Americans by purchasing troubled assets held by or on behalf of an eligible retirement plan described in clause (iii), (iv), (v), or (vi) of section 402(c)(8)(B) of the Internal Revenue Code of 1986, except that such authority shall not extend to any compensation arrangements subject to section 409A of such Code; and

(9) the utility of purchasing other real estate owned and instruments backed by mortgages on multifamily properties.

SEC. 104. FINANCIAL STABILITY OVERSIGHT BOARD.

(a) ESTABLISHMENT.—There is established the Financial Stability Oversight Board, which shall be responsible for—

(1) reviewing the exercise of authority under a program developed in accordance with this Act, including—

(A) policies implemented by the Secretary and the Office of Financial Stability created under sections 101 and 102, including the appointment of financial agents, the designation of asset classes to be purchased, and plans for the structure of vehicles used to purchase troubled assets; and

(B) the effect of such actions in assisting American families in preserving home ownership, stabilizing financial markets, and protecting taxpayers;

(2) making recommendations, as appropriate, to the Secretary regarding use of the authority under this Act; and

(3) reporting any suspected fraud, misrepresentation, or malfeasance to the Special Inspector General for the Troubled Assets Relief Program or the Attorney General of the United States, consistent with section 535(b) of title 28, United States Code.

(b) MEMBERSHIP.—The Financial Stability Oversight Board shall be comprised of—

(1) the Chairman of the Board of Governors of the Federal Reserve System;

(2) the Secretary;

(3) the Director of the Federal Housing Finance Agency;

(4) the Chairman of the Securities Exchange Commission; and

(5) the Secretary of Housing and Urban Development.

(c) CHAIRPERSON.—The chairperson of the Financial Stability Oversight Board shall be elected by the members of the Board from among the members other than the Secretary.

(d) MEETINGS.—The Financial Stability Oversight Board shall meet 2 weeks after the first exercise of the purchase authority of the Secretary under this Act, and monthly thereafter.

(e) ADDITIONAL AUTHORITIES.—In addition to the responsibilities described in subsection (a), the Financial Stability Oversight Board shall have the authority to ensure that the policies implemented by the Secretary are—

(1) in accordance with the purposes of this Act;

(2) in the economic interests of the United States; and

(3) consistent with protecting taxpayers, in accordance with section 113(a).

(f) CREDIT REVIEW COMMITTEE.—The Financial Stability Oversight Board may appoint a credit review committee for the purpose of evaluating the exercise of the purchase authority provided under this Act and the assets acquired through the exercise of such authority, as the Financial Stability Oversight Board determines appropriate.

(g) REPORTS.—The Financial Stability Oversight Board shall report to the appropriate committees of Congress and the Congressional Oversight Panel established under section 125, not less frequently than quarterly, on the matters described under subsection (a)(1).

(h) TERMINATION.—The Financial Stability Oversight Board, and its authority under this section, shall terminate on the expiration of the 15-day period beginning upon the later of—

(1) the date that the last troubled asset acquired by the Secretary under section 101 has been sold or transferred out of the ownership or control of the Federal Government; or

(2) the date of expiration of the last insurance contract issued under section 102.

SEC. 105. REPORTS.

(a) IN GENERAL.—Before the expiration of the 60-day period beginning on the date of the first exercise of the authority granted in section 101(a), or of the first exercise of the authority granted in section 102, whichever occurs first, and every 30-day period thereafter, the Secretary shall report to the appropriate committees of Congress, with respect to each such period—

(1) an overview of actions taken by the Secretary, including the considerations required by section 103 and the efforts under section 109;

(2) the actual obligation and expenditure of the funds provided for administrative expenses by section 118 during such period and the expected expenditure of such funds in the subsequent period; and

(3) a detailed financial statement with respect to the exercise of authority under this Act, including—

(A) all agreements made or renewed;

(B) all insurance contracts entered into pursuant to section 102;

(C) all transactions occurring during such period, including the types of parties involved;

(D) the nature of the assets purchased;

(E) all projected costs and liabilities;

(F) operating expenses, including compensation for financial agents;

(G) the valuation or pricing method used for each transaction; and

(H) a description of the vehicles established to exercise such authority.

(b) TRANCHE REPORTS TO CONGRESS.—

(1) REPORTS.—The Secretary shall provide to the appropriate committees of Congress, at the times specified in paragraph (2), a written report, including—

(A) a description of all of the transactions made during the reporting period;

(B) a description of the pricing mechanism for the transactions;

(C) a justification of the price paid for and other financial terms associated with the transactions;

(D) a description of the impact of the exercise of such authority on the financial system, supported, to the extent possible, by specific data;

(E) a description of challenges that remain in the financial system, including any benchmarks yet to be achieved; and

(F) an estimate of additional actions under the authority provided under this Act that may be necessary to address such challenges.

(2) TIMING.—The report required by this sub section shall be submitted not later than 7 days after the date on which commitments to purchase troubled assets under the authorities provided in this Act first reach an aggregate of $50,000,000,000 and not later than 7 days after each $50,000,000,000 interval of such commitments is reached thereafter.

(c) REGULATORY MODERNIZATION REPORT.—The Secretary shall review the current state of the financial markets and the regulatory system and submit a written report to the appropriate committees of Congress not later than April 30, 2009, analyzing the current state of the regulatory system and its effectiveness at overseeing the participants in the financial markets, including the over-the-counter swaps market and government-sponsored enterprises, and providing recommendations for improvement, including—

    (1) recommendations regarding—

        (A) whether any participants in the financial markets that are currently outside the regulatory system should become subject to the regulatory system; and

        (B) enhancement of the clearing and settlement of over-the-counter swaps; and

    (2) the rationale underlying such recommendations.

    (d) SHARING OF INFORMATION.—Any report required under this section shall also be submitted to the Congressional Oversight Panel established under section 125.

    (e) SUNSET.—The reporting requirements under this section shall terminate on the later of—

    (1) the date that the last troubled asset acquired by the Secretary under section 101 has been sold or transferred out of the ownership or control of the Federal Government; or

    (2) the date of expiration of the last insurance contract issued under section 102.

SEC. 106. RIGHTS; MANAGEMENT; SALE OF TROUBLED ASSETS; REVENUES AND SALE PROCEEDS.

    (a) EXERCISE OF RIGHTS.—The Secretary may, at any time, exercise any rights received in connection with troubled assets purchased under this Act.

    (b) MANAGEMENT OF TROUBLED ASSETS.—The Secretary shall have authority to manage troubled assets purchased under this Act, including revenues and portfolio risks therefrom.

    (c) SALE OF TROUBLED ASSETS.—The Secretary may, at any time, upon terms and conditions and at a price determined by the Secretary, sell, or enter into securities loans, repurchase transactions, or other financial transactions in regard to, any troubled asset purchased under this Act.

    (d) TRANSFER TO TREASURY.—Revenues of, and proceeds from the sale of troubled assets purchased under this Act, or from the sale, exercise, or surrender of warrants or senior debt instruments acquired under section 113 shall be paid into the general fund of the Treasury for reduction of the public debt.

    (e) APPLICATION OF SUNSET TO TROUBLED ASSETS.—The authority of the Secretary to hold any troubled asset purchased under this Act before the termination date in section 120, or to purchase or fund the purchase of a troubled asset under a commitment entered into before the termination date in section 120, is not subject to the provisions of section 120.

SEC. 107. CONTRACTING PROCEDURES.

(a) STREAMLINED PROCESS.—For purposes of this Act, the Secretary may waive specific provisions of the Federal Acquisition Regulation upon a determination that urgent and compelling circumstances make compliance with such provisions contrary to the public interest. Any such determination, and the justification for such determination, shall be submitted to the Committees on Oversight and Government Reform and Financial Services of the House of Representatives and the Committees on Homeland Security and Governmental Affairs and Banking, Housing, and Urban Affairs of the Senate within 7 days.

(b) ADDITIONAL CONTRACTING REQUIREMENTS.—In any solicitation or contract where the Secretary has, pursuant to subsection (a), waived any provision of the Federal Acquisition Regulation pertaining to minority contracting, the Secretary shall develop and implement standards and procedures to ensure, to the maximum extent practicable, the inclusion and utilization of minorities (as such term is defined in section 1204(c) of the Financial Institutions Reform, Recovery, and Enforcement Act of 1989 (12 U.S.C. 1811 note)) and women, and minority- and women-owned businesses (as such terms are defined in section 21A(r)(4) of the Federal Home Loan Bank Act (12 U.S.C. 1441a(r)(4)), in that solicitation or contract, including contracts to asset managers, servicers, property managers, and other service providers or expert consultants.

(c) ELIGIBILITY OF FDIC.—Notwithstanding subsections (a) and (b), the Corporation—

(1) shall be eligible for, and shall be considered in, the selection of asset managers for residential mortgage loans and residential mortgage-backed securities; and

(2) shall be reimbursed by the Secretary for any services provided.

SEC. 108. CONFLICTS OF INTEREST.

(a) STANDARDS REQUIRED.—The Secretary shall issue regulations or guidelines necessary to address and manage or to prohibit conflicts of interest that may arise in connection with the administration and execution of the authorities provided under this Act, including—

(1) conflicts arising in the selection or hiring of contractors or advisors, including asset managers;

(2) the purchase of troubled assets;

(3) the management of the troubled assets held;

(4) post-employment restrictions on employees; and

(5) any other potential conflict of interest, as the Secretary deems necessary or appropriate in the public interest.

(b) TIMING.—Regulations or guidelines required by this section shall be issued as soon as practicable after the date of enactment of this Act.

SEC. 109. FORECLOSURE MITIGATION EFFORTS.

(a) RESIDENTIAL MORTGAGE LOAN SERVICING STANDARDS.—To the extent that the Secretary acquires mortgages, mortgage backed securities, and other assets secured by residential real estate, including multi-family housing, the Secretary shall implement a plan that seeks to maximize assistance for homeowners and use the authority of the Secretary to encourage the servicers of the underlying mortgages, considering net present value to the taxpayer, to take advantage of the HOPE for Homeowners Program under section 257 of the National Housing Act or other available programs to minimize foreclosures. In addition, the Secretary may use loan guarantees and credit enhancements to facilitate loan modifications to prevent avoidable foreclosures.

(b) COORDINATION.—The Secretary shall coordinate with the Corporation, the Board (with respect to any mortgage or mortgage-backed securities or pool of securities held, owned, or controlled by or on behalf of a Federal reserve bank, as provided in section 110(a)(1)(C)), the Federal Housing Finance Agency, the Secretary of Housing and Urban Development, and other Federal Government entities that hold troubled assets to attempt to identify opportunities for the acquisition of classes of troubled assets that will improve the ability of the Secretary to improve the loan modification and restructuring process and, where permissible, to permit bona fide tenants who are current on their rent to remain in their homes under the terms of the lease. In the case of a mortgage on a residential rental property, the plan required under this section shall include protecting Federal, State, and local rental subsidies and protections, and ensuring any modification takes into account the need for operating funds to maintain decent and safe conditions at the property.

(c) CONSENT TO REASONABLE LOAN MODIFICATION REQUESTS.—Upon any request arising under existing investment contracts, the Secretary shall consent, where appropriate, and considering net present value to the taxpayer, to reasonable requests for loss mitigation measures, including term extensions, rate reductions, principal write downs, increases in the proportion of loans within a trust or other structure allowed to be modified, or removal of other limitation on modifications.

SEC. 110. ASSISTANCE TO HOMEOWNERS.

(a) DEFINITIONS.—As used in this section—
    (1) the term "Federal property manager" means—

(A) the Federal Housing Finance Agency, in its capacity as conservator of the Federal National Mortgage Association and the Federal Home Loan Mortgage Corporation;

(B) the Corporation, with respect to residential mortgage loans and mortgage-backed securities held by any bridge depository institution pursuant to section 11(n) of the Federal Deposit Insurance Act; and

(C) the Board, with respect to any mortgage or mortgage-backed securities or pool of securities held, owned, or controlled by or on behalf of a Federal reserve bank, other than mortgages or securities held, owned, or controlled in connection with open market operations under section 14 of the Federal Reserve Act (12 U.S.C. 353), or as collateral for an advance or discount that is not in default;

(2) the term "consumer" has the same meaning as in section 103 of the Truth in Lending Act (15 U.S.C. 1602);

(3) the term "insured depository institution" has the same meaning as in section 3 of the Federal Deposit Insurance Act (12 U.S.C. 1813); and

(4) the term "servicer" has the same meaning as in section 6(i)(2) of the Real Estate Settlement Procedures Act of 1974 (12 U.S.C. 2605(i)(2)).

(b) HOMEOWNER ASSISTANCE BY AGENCIES.—

(1) IN GENERAL.—To the extent that the Federal property manager holds, owns, or controls mortgages, mortgage backed securities, and other assets secured by residential real estate, including multifamily housing, the Federal property manager shall implement a plan that seeks to maximize assistance for homeowners and use its authority to encourage the servicers of the underlying mortgages, and considering net present value to the taxpayer, to take advantage of the HOPE for Homeowners Program under section 257 of the National Housing Act or other available programs to minimize foreclosures.

(2) MODIFICATIONS.—In the case of a residential mortgage loan, modifications made under paragraph (1) may include—

(A) reduction in interest rates;

(B) reduction of loan principal; and

(C) other similar modifications.

(3) TENANT PROTECTIONS.—In the case of mortgages on residential rental properties, modifications made under paragraph (1) shall ensure—

(A) the continuation of any existing Federal, State, and local rental subsidies and protections; and

(B) that modifications take into account the need for operating funds to maintain decent and safe conditions at the property.

(4) TIMING.—Each Federal property manager shall develop and begin implementation of the plan required by this subsection not later than 60 days after the date of enactment of this Act.

(5) REPORTS TO CONGRESS.—Each Federal property manager shall, 60 days after the date of enactment of this Act and every 30 days thereafter, report to Congress specific information on the number and types of loan modifications made and the number of actual foreclosures occurring during the reporting period in accordance with this section.

(6) CONSULTATION.—In developing the plan required by this subsection, the Federal property managers shall consult with one another and, to the extent possible, utilize consistent approaches to implement the requirements of this subsection.

(c) ACTIONS WITH RESPECT TO SERVICERS.—In any case in which a Federal property manager is not the owner of a residential mortgage loan, but holds an interest in obligations or pools of obligations secured by residential mortgage loans, the Federal property manager shall—

(1) encourage implementation by the loan servicers of loan modifications developed under subsection (b); and

(2) assist in facilitating any such modifications, to the extent possible.

(d) LIMITATION.—The requirements of this section shall not supersede any other duty or requirement imposed on the Federal property managers under otherwise applicable law.

SEC. 111. EXECUTIVE COMPENSATION AND CORPORATE GOVERNANCE.

(a) APPLICABILITY.—Any financial institution that sells troubled assets to the Secretary under this Act shall be subject to the executive compensation requirements of subsections (b) and (c) and the provisions under the Internal Revenue Code of 1986, as provided under the amendment by section 302, as applicable.

(b) DIRECT PURCHASES.—

(1) IN GENERAL.—Where the Secretary determines that the purposes of this Act are best met through direct purchases of troubled assets from an individual financial institution where no bidding process or market prices are available, and the Secretary receives a meaningful equity or debt position in the financial institution as a result of the transaction, the Secretary shall require that the financial institution meet appropriate standards for executive compensation and corporate governance. The standards required under this subsection shall be effective for the duration of the period that the Secretary holds an equity or debt position in the financial institution.

(2) CRITERIA.—The standards required under this subsection shall include—

(A) limits on compensation that exclude incentives for senior executive officers of a financial institution to take unnecessary and excessive risks that threaten the value of the financial institution during the period that the Secretary holds an equity or debt position in the financial institution;

(B) a provision for the recovery by the financial institution of any bonus or incentive compensation paid to a senior executive officer based on statements of earnings, gains, or other criteria that are later proven to be materially inaccurate; and

(C) a prohibition on the financial institution making any golden parachute payment to its senior executive officer during the period that the Secretary holds an equity or debt position in the financial institution.

(3) DEFINITION.—For purposes of this section, the term "senior executive officer" means an individual who is one of the top 5 highly paid executives of a public company, whose compensation is required to be disclosed pursuant to the Securities Exchange Act of 1934, and any regulations issued thereunder, and non-public company counterparts.

(c) AUCTION PURCHASES.—Where the Secretary determines that the purposes of this Act are best met through auction purchases of troubled assets, and only where such purchases per financial institution in the aggregate exceed $300,000,000 (including direct purchases), the Secretary shall prohibit, for such financial institution, any new employment contract with a senior executive officer that provides a golden parachute in the event of an involuntary termination, bankruptcy filing, insolvency, or receivership. The Secretary shall issue guidance to carry out this paragraph not later than 2 months after the date of enactment of this Act, and such guidance shall be effective upon issuance.

(d) SUNSET.—The provisions of subsection (c) shall apply only to arrangements entered into during the period during which the authorities under section 101(a) are in effect, as determined under section 120.

SEC. 112. COORDINATION WITH FOREIGN AUTHORITIES AND CENTRAL BANKS.

The Secretary shall coordinate, as appropriate, with foreign financial authorities and central banks to work toward the establishment of similar programs by such authorities and central banks. To the extent that such foreign financial authorities or banks hold troubled assets as a result of extending financing to financial institutions that have failed or defaulted on such financing, such troubled assets qualify for purchase under section 101.

SEC. 113. MINIMIZATION OF LONG-TERM COSTS AND MAXIMIZATION OF BENEFITS FOR TAXPAYERS.

(a) LONG-TERM COSTS AND BENEFITS.—

(1) MINIMIZING NEGATIVE IMPACT.—The Secretary shall use the authority under this Act in a manner that will minimize any potential long-term negative impact on the taxpayer, taking into account the direct outlays, potential long-term returns on assets purchased, and the overall economic benefits of the program, including economic benefits due to improvements in economic activity and the availability of credit, the impact on the savings and pensions of individuals, and reductions in losses to the Federal Government.

(2) AUTHORITY.—In carrying out paragraph (1), the Secretary shall—

(A) hold the assets to maturity or for resale for and until such time as the Secretary determines that the market is optimal for selling such assets, in order to maximize the value for taxpayers; and

(B) sell such assets at a price that the Secretary determines, based on available financial analysis, will maximize return on investment for the Federal Government.

(3) PRIVATE SECTOR PARTICIPATION.—The Secretary shall encourage the private sector to participate in purchases of troubled assets, and to invest in financial institutions, consistent with the provisions of this section.

(b) USE OF MARKET MECHANISMS.—In making purchases under this Act, the Secretary shall—

(1) make such purchases at the lowest price that the Secretary determines to be consistent with the purposes of this Act; and

(2) maximize the efficiency of the use of taxpayer resources by using market mechanisms, including auctions or reverse auctions, where appropriate.

(c) DIRECT PURCHASES.—If the Secretary determines that use of a market mechanism under subsection (b) is not feasible or appropriate, and the purposes of the Act are best met through direct purchases from an individual financial institution, the Secretary shall pursue additional measures to ensure that prices paid for assets are reasonable and reflect the underlying value of the asset.

(d) CONDITIONS ON PURCHASE AUTHORITY FOR WARRANTS AND DEBT INSTRUMENTS.—

(1) IN GENERAL.—The Secretary may not purchase, or make any commitment to purchase, any troubled asset under the authority of this Act, unless the Secretary receives from the financial institution from which such assets are to be purchased—

(A) in the case of a financial institution, the securities of which are traded on a national securities exchange, a warrant giving the right to the Secretary to receive nonvoting common stock or preferred stock in such financial institution, or voting stock with respect to which, the Secretary agrees not to exercise voting power, as the Secretary determines appropriate; or

(B) in the case of any financial institution other than one described in subparagraph (A), a warrant for common or preferred stock, or a senior debt instrument from such financial institution, as described in paragraph (2)(C).

(2) TERMS AND CONDITIONS.—The terms and conditions of any warrant or senior debt instrument required under paragraph (1) shall meet the following requirements:

(A) PURPOSES.—Such terms and conditions shall, at a minimum, be designed—

(i) to provide for reasonable participation by the Secretary, for the benefit of taxpayers, in equity appreciation in the case of a warrant or other equity security, or a reasonable interest rate premium, in the case of a debt instrument; and

(ii) to provide additional protection for the taxpayer against losses from sale of assets by the Secretary under this Act and the administrative expenses of the TARP.

(B) AUTHORITY TO SELL, EXERCISE, OR SURRENDER.—The Secretary may sell, exercise, or surrender a warrant or any senior debt instrument received under this subsection, based on the conditions established under subparagraph (A).

(C) CONVERSION.—The warrant shall provide that if, after the warrant is received by the Secretary under this subsection, the financial institution that issued the warrant is no longer listed or traded on a national securities exchange or securities association, as described in paragraph (1)(A), such warrants shall convert to senior debt, or contain appropriate protections for the Secretary to ensure that the Treasury is appropriately compensated for the value of the warrant, in an amount determined by the Secretary.

(D) PROTECTIONS.—Any warrant representing securities to be received by the Secretary under this subsection shall contain antidilution provisions of the type employed in capital market transactions, as determined by the Secretary. Such provisions shall protect the value of the securities from market transactions such as stock splits, stock distributions, dividends, and other distributions, mergers, and other forms of reorganization or recapitalization.

(E) EXERCISE PRICE.—The exercise price for any warrant issued pursuant to this subsection shall be set by the Secretary, in the interest of the taxpayers.

(F) SUFFICIENCY.—The financial institution shall guarantee to the Secretary that it has authorized shares of nonvoting stock available to fulfill its obligations under this subsection. Should the financial institution not have sufficient authorized shares, including preferred shares that may carry dividend rights equal to a multiple number of common shares, the Secretary may, to the extent necessary, accept a senior debt note in an amount, and on such terms as will compensate the Secretary with equivalent value, in the event that a sufficient shareholder vote to authorize the necessary additional shares cannot be obtained.

(3) EXCEPTIONS.—

(A) DE MINIMIS.—The Secretary shall establish de minimis exceptions to the requirements of this subsection, based on the size of the cumulative transactions of troubled assets purchased from any one financial institution for the duration of the program, at not more than $100,000,000.

(B) OTHER EXCEPTIONS.—The Secretary shall establish an exception to the requirements of this subsection and appropriate alternative requirements for any participating financial institution that is legally prohibited from issuing securities and debt instruments, so as not to allow circumvention of the requirements of this section.

SEC. 114. MARKET TRANSPARENCY.

(a) PRICING.—To facilitate market transparency, the Secretary shall make available to the public, in electronic form, a description, amounts, and pricing of assets acquired under this Act, within 2 business days of purchase, trade, or other disposition.

(b) DISCLOSURE.—For each type of financial institutions that sells troubled assets to the Secretary under this Act, the Secretary shall determine whether the public disclosure required for such financial institutions with respect to off-balance sheet transactions, derivatives instruments, contingent liabilities, and similar sources of potential exposure is adequate to provide to the public sufficient information as to the true financial position of the institutions. If such disclosure is not adequate for that purpose, the Secretary shall make recommendations for additional disclosure requirements to the relevant regulators.

SEC. 115. GRADUATED AUTHORIZATION TO PURCHASE.

(a) AUTHORITY.—The authority of the Secretary to purchase troubled assets under this Act shall be limited as follows:

(1) Effective upon the date of enactment of this Act, such authority shall be limited to $250,000,000,000 outstanding at any one time.

(2) If at any time, the President submits to the Congress a written certification that the Secretary needs to exercise the authority under this paragraph, effective upon such submission, such authority shall be limited to $350,000,000,000 outstanding at any one time.

(3) If, at any time after the certification in paragraph (2) has been made, the President transmits to the Congress a written report detailing the plan of the Secretary to exercise the authority under this paragraph, unless there is enacted, within 15 calendar days of such transmission, a joint resolution described in subsection (c), effective upon the expiration of such 15-day period, such authority shall be limited to $700,000,000,000 outstanding at any one time.

(b) AGGREGATION OF PURCHASE PRICES.—The amount of troubled assets purchased by the Secretary out-standing at any one time shall be determined for purposes of the dollar amount limitations under subsection (a) by aggregating the purchase prices of all troubled assets held.

(c) JOINT RESOLUTION OF DISAPPROVAL.—

(1) IN GENERAL.—Notwithstanding any other provision of this section, the Secretary may not exercise any authority to make purchases under this Act with regard to any amount in excess of $350,000,000,000 previously obligated, as described in this section if, within 15 calendar days after the date on which Congress receives a report of the plan of the Secretary described in subsection (a)(3), there is enacted into law a joint resolution disapproving the plan of the Secretary with respect to such additional amount.

(2) CONTENTS OF JOINT RESOLUTION.—For the purpose of this section, the term "joint resolution" means only a joint resolution—

(A) that is introduced not later than 3 calendar days after the date on which the report of the plan of the Secretary referred to in subsection (a)(3) is received by Congress;

(B) which does not have a preamble;

(C) the title of which is as follows: "Joint resolution relating to the disapproval of obligations under the Emergency Economic Stabilization Act of 2008"; and

(D) the matter after the resolving clause of which is as follows: "That Congress disapproves the obligation of any amount exceeding the amounts obligated as described in paragraphs (1) and (2) of section 115(a) of the Emergency Economic Stabilization Act of 2008."

(d) FAST TRACK CONSIDERATION IN HOUSE OF REPRESENTATIVES.—

(1) RECONVENING.—Upon receipt of a report under subsection (a)(3), the Speaker, if the House would otherwise be adjourned, shall notify the Members of the House that, pursuant to this

section, the House shall convene not later than the second calendar day after receipt of such report;

(2) REPORTING AND DISCHARGE.—Any committee of the House of Representatives to which a joint resolution is referred shall report it to the House not later than 5 calendar days after the date of receipt of the report described in subsection (a)(3). If a committee fails to report the joint resolution within that period, the committee shall be discharged from further consideration of the joint resolution and the joint resolution shall be referred to the appropriate calendar.

(3) PROCEEDING TO CONSIDERATION.—After each committee authorized to consider a joint resolution reports it to the House or has been discharged from its consideration, it shall be in order, not later than the sixth day after Congress receives the report described in subsection (a)(3), to move to proceed to consider the joint resolution in the House. All points of order against the motion are waived. Such a motion shall not be in order after the House has disposed of a motion to proceed on the joint resolution. The previous question shall be considered as ordered on the motion to its adoption without intervening motion. The motion shall not be debatable. A motion to reconsider the vote by which the motion is disposed of shall not be in order.

(4) CONSIDERATION.—The joint resolution shall be considered as read. All points of order against the joint resolution and against its consideration are waived. The previous question shall be considered as ordered on the joint resolution to its passage without intervening motion except two hours of debate equally divided and controlled by the proponent and an opponent. A motion to reconsider the vote on passage of the joint resolution shall not be in order.

(e) FAST TRACK CONSIDERATION IN SENATE.—

(1) RECONVENING.—Upon receipt of a report under subsection (a)(3), if the Senate has adjourned or recessed for more than 2 days, the majority leader of the Senate, after consultation with the minority leader of the Senate, shall notify the Members of the Senate that, pursuant to this section, the Senate shall convene not later than the second calendar day after receipt of such message.

(2) PLACEMENT ON CALENDAR.—Upon introduction in the Senate, the joint resolution shall be placed immediately on the calendar.

(3) FLOOR CONSIDERATION.—

(A) IN GENERAL.—Notwithstanding Rule XXII of the Standing Rules of the Senate, it is in order at any time during the period beginning on the 4th day after the date on which Congress receives a report of the plan of the Secretary described in subsection (a)(3) and ending on the 6th day after the date on which Congress receives a report of the plan of the Secretary described in subsection (a)(3) (even though a previous motion to the same effect has been disagreed to) to move to proceed to the consideration of the joint resolution, and all points of order against the joint resolution (and against consideration of the joint resolution) are waived. The motion to proceed is not debatable. The motion is not subject to a motion to postpone. A motion to reconsider the vote by which the motion is agreed to or disagreed to shall not be in order. If a motion to proceed to the consideration of the resolution is agreed to, the joint resolution shall remain the unfinished business until disposed of.

(B) DEBATE.—Debate on the joint resolution, and on all debatable motions and appeals in connection therewith, shall be limited to not more than 10 hours, which shall be divided equally between the majority and minority leaders or their designees. A motion further to limit debate is in order and not debatable. An amendment to, or a motion to postpone, or a motion to proceed to the consideration of other business, or a motion to recommit the joint resolution is not in order.

(C) VOTE ON PASSAGE.—The vote on passage shall occur immediately following the conclusion of the debate on a joint resolution, and a single quorum call at the conclusion of the debate if requested in accordance with the rules of the Senate.

(D) RULINGS OF THE CHAIR ON PROCEDURE.—Appeals from the decisions of the Chair relating to the application of the rules of the Senate, as the case may be, to the procedure relating to a joint resolution shall be decided without debate.

(f) RULES RELATING TO SENATE AND HOUSE OF REPRESENTATIVES.—

(1) COORDINATION WITH ACTION BY OTHER HOUSE.—If, before the passage by one House of a joint resolution of that House, that House receives from the other House a joint resolution, then the following procedures shall apply:

(A) The joint resolution of the other House shall not be referred to a committee.

(B) With respect to a joint resolution of the House receiving the resolution—

(i) the procedure in that House shall be the same as if no joint resolution had been received from the other House; but

(ii) the vote on passage shall be on the joint resolution of the other House.

(2) TREATMENT OF JOINT RESOLUTION OF OTHER HOUSE.—If one House fails to introduce or consider a joint resolution under this section, the joint resolution of the other House shall be entitled to expedited floor procedures under this section.

(3) TREATMENT OF COMPANION MEASURES.—If, following passage of the joint resolution in the Senate, the Senate then receives the companion measure from the House of Representatives, the companion measure shall not be debatable.

(4) CONSIDERATION AFTER PASSAGE.—

(A) IN GENERAL.—If Congress passes a joint resolution, the period beginning on the date the President is presented with the joint resolution and ending on the date the President takes action with respect to the joint resolution shall be disregarded in computing the 15-calendar day period described in subsection (a)(3).

(B) VETOES.—If the President vetoes the joint resolution—

(i) the period beginning on the date the President vetoes the joint resolution and ending on the date the Congress receives the veto message with respect to the joint resolution shall be disregarded in computing the 15-calendar day period described in subsection (a)(3), and

(ii) debate on a veto message in the Senate under this section shall be 1 hour equally divided between the majority and minority leaders or their designees.

(5) RULES OF HOUSE OF REPRESENTATIVES AND SENATE.—This subsection and subsections (c), (d), and (e) are enacted by Congress—

(A) as an exercise of the rulemaking power of the Senate and House of Representatives, respectively, and as such it is deemed a part of the rules of each House, respectively, but applicable only with respect to the procedure to be followed in that House in the case of a joint resolution, and it supersedes other rules only to the extent that it is inconsistent with such rules; and

(B) with full recognition of the constitutional right of either House to change the rules (so far as relating to the procedure of that House) at any time, in the same manner, and to the same extent as in the case of any other rule of that House.

SEC. 116. OVERSIGHT AND AUDITS.

(a) COMPTROLLER GENERAL OVERSIGHT.—

(1) SCOPE OF OVERSIGHT.—The Comptroller General of the United States shall, upon establishment of the troubled assets relief program under this Act (in this section referred to as the "TARP"), commence ongoing oversight of the activities and performance of the TARP and of any agents and representatives of the TARP (as related to the agent or representative's activities on behalf of or under the authority of the TARP), including vehicles

established by the Secretary under this Act. The subjects of such oversight shall include the following:

(A) The performance of the TARP in meeting the purposes of this Act, particularly those involving—

(i) foreclosure mitigation;

(ii) cost reduction;

(iii) whether it has provided stability or prevented disruption to the financial markets or the banking system; and

(iv) whether it has protected taxpayers.

(B) The financial condition and internal controls of the TARP, its representatives and agents.

(C) Characteristics of transactions and commitments entered into, including transaction type, frequency, size, prices paid, and all other relevant terms and conditions, and the timing, duration and terms of any future commitments to purchase assets.

(D) Characteristics and disposition of acquired assets, including type, acquisition price, current market value, sale prices and terms, and use of proceeds from sales.

(E) Efficiency of the operations of the TARP in the use of appropriated funds.

(F) Compliance with all applicable laws and regulations by the TARP, its agents and representatives.

(G) The efforts of the TARP to prevent, identify, and minimize conflicts of interest involving any agent or representative performing activities on behalf of or under the authority of the TARP.

(H) The efficacy of contracting procedures pursuant to section 107(b), including, as applicable, the efforts of the TARP in evaluating proposals for inclusion and contracting to the maximum extent possible of minorities (as such term is defined in 1204(c) of the Financial Institutions Reform, Recovery, and Enhancement Act of 1989 (12 U.S.C. 1811 note), women, and minority- and women-owned businesses, including ascertaining and reporting the total amount of fees paid and other value delivered by the TARP to all of its agents and representatives, and such amounts paid or delivered to such firms that are minority- and women-owned businesses (as such terms are defined in section 21A of the Federal Home Loan Bank Act (12 U.S.C. 1441a)).

(2) CONDUCT AND ADMINISTRATION OF OVERSIGHT.—

(A) GAO PRESENCE.—The Secretary shall provide the Comptroller General with appropriate space and facilities in the Department of the Treasury as necessary to facilitate oversight of the TARP until the termination date established in section 120.

(B) ACCESS TO RECORDS.—To the extent otherwise consistent with law, the Comptroller General shall have access, upon request, to any information, data, schedules, books, accounts, financial records, reports, files, electronic communications, or other papers, things, or property belonging to or in use by the TARP, or any vehicles established by the Secretary under this Act, and to the officers, directors, employees, independent public accountants, financial advisors, and other agents and representatives of the TARP (as related to the agent or representative's activities on behalf of or under the authority of the TARP) or any such vehicle at such reasonable time as the Comptroller General may request. The Comptroller General shall be afforded full facilities for verifying transactions with the balances or securities held by depositaries, fiscal agents, and custodians. The Comptroller General may make and retain copies of such books, accounts, and other records as the Comptroller General deems appropriate.

(C) REIMBURSEMENT OF COSTS.—The Treasury shall reimburse the Government Accountability Office for the full cost of any such oversight activities as billed therefor by the Comptroller General of the United States. Such reimbursements shall be credited to the appropriation account "Salaries and Expenses, Government Accountability Office" current when the payment is received and remain available until expended.

(3) REPORTING.—The Comptroller General shall submit reports of findings under this section, regularly and no less frequently than once every 60 days, to the appropriate committees of Congress, and the Special Inspector General for the Troubled Asset Relief Program established under this Act on the activities and performance of the TARP. The Comptroller may also submit special reports under this subsection as warranted by the findings of its oversight activities.

(b) COMPTROLLER GENERAL AUDITS.—

(1) ANNUAL AUDIT.—The TARP shall annually prepare and issue to the appropriate committees of Congress and the public audited financial statements prepared in accordance with generally accepted accounting principles, and the Comptroller General shall annually audit such statements in accordance with generally accepted auditing standards. The Treasury shall reimburse the Government Accountability Office for the full cost of any such audit as billed therefor by the Comptroller General. Such reimbursements

shall be credited to the appropriation account "Salaries and Expenses, Government Accountability Office" current when the payment is received and remain available until expended. The financial statements prepared under this paragraph shall be on the fiscal year basis prescribed under section 1102 of title 31, United States Code.

(2) AUTHORITY.—The Comptroller General may audit the programs, activities, receipts, expenditures, and financial transactions of the TARP and any agents and representatives of the TARP (as related to the agent or representative's activities on behalf of or under the authority of the TARP), including vehicles established by the Secretary under this Act.

(3) CORRECTIVE RESPONSES TO AUDIT PROBLEMS.—The TARP shall—

(A) take action to address deficiencies identified by the Comptroller General or other auditor engaged by the TARP; or

(B) certify to appropriate committees of Congress that no action is necessary or appropriate.

(c) INTERNAL CONTROL.—

(1) ESTABLISHMENT.—The TARP shall establish and maintain an effective system of internal control, consistent with the standards prescribed under section 3512(c) of title 31, United States Code, that provides reasonable assurance of—

(A) the effectiveness and efficiency of operations, including the use of the resources of the TARP;

(B) the reliability of financial reporting, including financial statements and other reports for internal and external use; and

(C) compliance with applicable laws and regulations.

(2) REPORTING.—In conjunction with each annual financial statement issued under this section, the TARP shall—

(A) state the responsibility of management for establishing and maintaining adequate internal control over financial reporting; and

(B) state its assessment, as of the end of the most recent year covered by such financial statement of the TARP, of the effectiveness of the internal control over financial reporting.

(d) SHARING OF INFORMATION.—Any report or audit required under this section shall also be submitted to the Congressional Oversight Panel established under section 125.

(e) TERMINATION.—Any oversight, reporting, or audit requirement under this section shall terminate on the later of—

(1) the date that the last troubled asset acquired by the Secretary under section 101 has been sold or transferred out of the ownership or control of the Federal Government; or

(2) the date of expiration of the last insurance contract issued under section 102.

SEC. 117. STUDY AND REPORT ON MARGIN AUTHORITY.

(a) STUDY.—The Comptroller General shall undertake a study to determine the extent to which leverage and sudden deleveraging of financial institutions was a factor behind the current financial crisis.

(b) CONTENT.—The study required by this section shall include—

(1) an analysis of the roles and responsibilities of the Board, the Securities and Exchange Commission, the Secretary, and other Federal banking agencies with respect to monitoring leverage and acting to curtail excessive leveraging;

(2) an analysis of the authority of the Board to regulate leverage, including by setting margin requirements, and what process the Board used to decide whether or not to use its authority;

(3) an analysis of any usage of the margin authority by the Board; and

(4) recommendations for the Board and appropriate committees of Congress with respect to the existing authority of the Board.

(c) REPORT.—Not later than June 1, 2009, the Comptroller General shall complete and submit a report on the study required by this section to the Committee on Banking, Housing, and Urban Affairs of the Senate and the Committee on Financial Services of the House of Representatives.

(d) SHARING OF INFORMATION.—Any reports required under this section shall also be submitted to the Congressional Oversight Panel established under section 125.

SEC. 118. FUNDING.

For the purpose of the authorities granted in this Act, and for the costs of administering those authorities, the Secretary may use the proceeds of the sale of any securities issued under chapter 31 of title 31, United States Code, and the purposes for which securities may be issued under chapter 31 of title 31, United States Code, are extended to include actions authorized by this Act, including the payment of administrative expenses. Any funds expended or obligated by the Secretary for actions authorized by this Act, including the payment of administrative expenses, shall be deemed appropriated at the time of such expenditure or obligation.

SEC. 119. JUDICIAL REVIEW AND RELATED MATTERS.

(a) JUDICIAL REVIEW.—

(1) STANDARD.—Actions by the Secretary pursuant to the authority of this Act shall be subject to chapter 7 of title 5, United

States Code, including that such final actions shall be held unlawful and set aside if found to be arbitrary, capricious, an abuse of discretion, or not in accordance with law.

(2) LIMITATIONS ON EQUITABLE RELIEF.—

(A) INJUNCTION.—No injunction or other form of equitable relief shall be issued against the Secretary for actions pursuant to section 101, 102, 106, and 109, other than to remedy a violation of the Constitution.

(B) TEMPORARY RESTRAINING ORDER.—Any request for a temporary restraining order against the Secretary for actions pursuant to this Act shall be considered and granted or denied by the court within 3 days of the date of the request.

(C) PRELIMINARY INJUNCTION.—Any request for a preliminary injunction against the Secretary for actions pursuant to this Act shall be considered and granted or denied by the court on an expedited basis consistent with the provisions of rule 65(b)(3) of the Federal Rules of Civil Procedure, or any successor thereto.

(D) PERMANENT INJUNCTION.—Any request for a permanent injunction against the Secretary for actions pursuant to this Act shall be considered and granted or denied by the court on an expedited basis. Whenever possible, the court shall consolidate trial on the merits with any hearing on a request for a preliminary injunction, consistent with the provisions of rule 65(a)(2) of the Federal Rules of Civil Procedure, or any successor thereto.

(3) LIMITATION ON ACTIONS BY PARTICIPATING COMPANIES.—No action or claims may be brought against the Secretary by any person that divests its assets with respect to its participation in a program under this Act, except as provided in paragraph (1), other than as expressly provided in a written contract with the Secretary.

(4) STAYS.—Any injunction or other form of equitable relief issued against the Secretary for ac tions pursuant to section 101, 102, 106, and 109, shall be automatically stayed. The stay shall be lifted unless the Secretary seeks a stay from a higher court within 3 calendar days after the date on which the relief is issued.

(b) RELATED MATTERS.—

(1) TREATMENT OF HOMEOWNERS' RIGHTS.— The terms of any residential mortgage loan that is part of any purchase by the Secretary under this Act shall remain subject to all claims and defenses that would otherwise apply, notwithstanding the exercise of authority by the Secretary under this Act.

(2) SAVINGS CLAUSE.—Any exercise of the authority of the Secretary pursuant to this Act shall not impair the claims or defenses that would otherwise apply with respect to persons other than the Secretary. Except as established in any contract, a servicer of

pooled residential mortgages owes any duty to determine whether the net present value of the payments on the loan, as modified, is likely to be greater than the anticipated net recovery that would result from foreclosure to all investors and holders of beneficial interests in such investment, but not to any individual or groups of investors or beneficial interest holders, and shall be deemed to act in the best interests of all such investors or holders of beneficial interests if the servicer agrees to or implements a modification or workout plan when the servicer takes reasonable loss mitigation actions, including partial payments.

SEC. 120. TERMINATION OF AUTHORITY.

(a) TERMINATION.—The authorities provided under sections 101(a), excluding section 101(a)(3), and 102 shall terminate on December 31, 2009.

(b) EXTENSION UPON CERTIFICATION.—The Secretary, upon submission of a written certification to Congress, may extend the authority provided under this Act to expire not later than 2 years from the date of enactment of this Act. Such certification shall include a justification of why the extension is necessary to assist American families and stabilize financial markets, as well as the expected cost to the taxpayers for such an extension.

SEC. 121. SPECIAL INSPECTOR GENERAL FOR THE TROUBLED ASSET RELIEF PROGRAM.

(a) OFFICE OF INSPECTOR GENERAL.—There is hereby established the Office of the Special Inspector General for the Troubled Asset Relief Program.

(b) APPOINTMENT OF INSPECTOR GENERAL; REMOVAL.—

(1) The head of the Office of the Special Inspector General for the Troubled Asset Relief Program is the Special Inspector General for the Troubled Asset Relief Program (in this section referred to as the "Special Inspector General"), who shall be appointed by the President, by and with the advice and consent of the Senate.

(2) The appointment of the Special Inspector General shall be made on the basis of integrity and demonstrated ability in accounting, auditing, financial analysis, law, management analysis, public administration, or investigations.

(3) The nomination of an individual as Special Inspector General shall be made as soon as practicable after the establishment of any program under sections 101 and 102.

(4) The Special Inspector General shall be removable from office in accordance with the provisions of section 3(b) of the Inspector General Act of 1978 (5 U.S.C. App.).

(5) For purposes of section 7324 of title 5, United States Code, the Special Inspector General shall not be considered an employee who determines policies to be pursued by the United States in the nationwide administration of Federal law.

(6) The annual rate of basic pay of the Special Inspector General shall be the annual rate of basic pay for an Inspector General under section 3(e) of the Inspector General Act of 1978 (5 U.S.C. App.).

(c) DUTIES.—

(1) It shall be the duty of the Special Inspector General to conduct, supervise, and coordinate audits and investigations of the purchase, management, and sale of assets by the Secretary of the Treasury under any program established by the Secretary under section 101, and the management by the Secretary of any program established under section 102, including by collecting and summarizing the following information:

(A) A description of the categories of troubled assets purchased or otherwise procured by the Secretary.

(B) A listing of the troubled assets purchased in each such category described under subparagraph (A).

(C) An explanation of the reasons the Secretary deemed it necessary to purchase each such troubled asset.

(D) A listing of each financial institution that such troubled assets were purchased from.

(E) A listing of and detailed biographical information on each person or entity hired to manage such troubled assets.

(F) A current estimate of the total amount of troubled assets purchased pursuant to any program established under section 101, the amount of troubled assets on the books of the Treasury, the amount of troubled assets sold, and the profit and loss incurred on each sale or disposition of each such troubled asset.

(G) A listing of the insurance contracts issued under section 102.

(2) The Special Inspector General shall establish, maintain, and oversee such systems, procedures, and controls as the Special Inspector General considers appropriate to discharge the duty under paragraph (1).

(3) In addition to the duties specified in paragraphs (1) and (2), the Inspector General shall also have the duties and responsibilities of inspectors general under the Inspector General Act of 1978.

(d) POWERS AND AUTHORITIES.—

(1) In carrying out the duties specified in subsection (c), the Special Inspector General shall have the authorities provided in section 6 of the Inspector General Act of 1978.

(2) The Special Inspector General shall carry out the duties specified in subsection (c)(1) in accordance with section 4(b)(1) of the Inspector General Act of 1978.

(e) PERSONNEL, FACILITIES, AND OTHER RESOURCES.—

(1) The Special Inspector General may select, appoint, and employ such officers and employees as may be necessary for carrying out the duties of the Special Inspector General, subject to the provisions of title 5, United States Code, governing appointments in the competitive service, and the provisions of chapter 51 and subchapter III of chapter 53 of such title, relating to classification and General Schedule pay rates.

(2) The Special Inspector General may obtain services as authorized by section 3109 of title 5, United States Code, at daily rates not to exceed the equivalent rate prescribed for grade GS–15 of the General Schedule by section 5332 of such title.

(3) The Special Inspector General may enter into contracts and other arrangements for audits, studies, analyses, and other services with public agencies and with private persons, and make such payments as may be necessary to carry out the duties of the Inspector General.

(4)(A) Upon request of the Special Inspector General for information or assistance from any department, agency, or other entity of the Federal Government, the head of such entity shall, insofar as is practicable and not in contravention of any existing law, furnish such information or assistance to the Special Inspector General, or an authorized designee.

(B) Whenever information or assistance requested by the Special Inspector General is, in the judgment of the Special Inspector General, unreasonably refused or not provided, the Special Inspector General shall report the circumstances to the appropriate committees of Congress without delay.

(f) REPORTS.—

(1) Not later than 60 days after the confirmation of the Special Inspector General, and every calendar quarter thereafter, the Special Inspector General shall submit to the appropriate committees of Congress a report summarizing the activities of the Special Inspector General during the 120-day period ending on the date of such report. Each report shall include, for the period covered by such report, a detailed statement of all purchases, obligations, expenditures, and revenues associated with any program established by the Secretary of the Treasury under sections 101 and 102, as well as the information collected under subsection (c)(1).

(2) Nothing in this subsection shall be construed to authorize the public disclosure of information that is—

(A) specifically prohibited from disclosure by any other provision of law;

(B) specifically required by Executive order to be protected from disclosure in the interest of national defense or national security or in the conduct of foreign affairs; or

(C) a part of an ongoing criminal investigation.

(3) Any reports required under this section shall also be submitted to the Congressional Oversight Panel established under section 125.

(g) FUNDING.—

(1) Of the amounts made available to the Secretary of the Treasury under section 118, $50,000,000 shall be available to the Special Inspector General to carry out this section.

(2) The amount available under paragraph (1) shall remain available until expended.

(h) TERMINATION.—The Office of the Special Inspector General shall terminate on the later of—

(1) the date that the last troubled asset acquired by the Secretary under section 101 has been sold or transferred out of the ownership or control of the Federal Government; or

(2) the date of expiration of the last insurance contract issued under section 102.

SEC. 122. INCREASE IN STATUTORY LIMIT ON THE PUBLIC DEBT.

Subsection (b) of section 3101 of title 31, United States Code, is amended by striking out the dollar limitation contained in such subsection and inserting "$11,315,000,000,000".

SEC. 123. CREDIT REFORM.

(a) IN GENERAL.—Subject to subsection (b), the costs of purchases of troubled assets made under section 101(a) and guarantees of troubled assets under section 102, and any cash flows associated with the activities authorized in section 102 and subsections (a), (b), and (c) of section 106 shall be determined as provided under the Federal Credit Reform Act of 1990 (2 U.S.C. 661 et. seq.), as applicable.

(b) COSTS.—For the purposes of section 502(5) of the Federal Credit Reform Act of 1990 (2 U.S.C. 661a(5))—

(1) the cost of troubled assets and guarantees of troubled assets shall be calculated by adjusting the discount rate in section 502(5)(E) (2 U.S.C. 661a(5)(E)) for market risks; and

(2) the cost of a modification of a troubled asset or guarantee of a troubled asset shall be the difference between the current estimate consistent with paragraph (1) under the terms of the troubled asset or guarantee of the troubled asset and the current estimate consistent with paragraph (1) under the terms of the troubled asset or guarantee of the troubled asset, as modified.

SEC. 124. HOPE FOR HOMEOWNERS AMENDMENTS.

Section 257 of the National Housing Act (12 U.S.C. 1715z-23) is amended—
    (1) in subsection (e)—
        (A) in paragraph (1)(B), by inserting before "a ratio" the following: ", or thereafter is likely to have, due to the terms of the mortgage being reset,";
        (B) in paragraph (2)(B), by inserting before the period at the end "(or such higher percentage as the Board determines, in the discretion of the Board)";
        (C) in paragraph (4)(A)—
            (i) in the first sentence, by inserting after "insured loan" the following: "and any payments made under this paragraph,"; and
            (ii) by adding at the end the following: "Such actions may include making payments, which shall be accepted as payment in full of all indebtedness under the eligible mortgage, to any holder of an existing subordinate mortgage, in lieu of any future appreciation payments authorized under subparagraph (B)."; and
    (2) in subsection (w), by inserting after "administrative costs" the following: "and payments pursuant to subsection (e)(4)(A)".

SEC. 125. CONGRESSIONAL OVERSIGHT PANEL.

    (a) ESTABLISHMENT.—There is hereby established the Congressional Oversight Panel (hereafter in this section referred to as the "Oversight Panel") as an establishment in the legislative branch.
    (b) DUTIES.—The Oversight Panel shall review the current state of the financial markets and the regulatory system and submit the following reports to Congress:
    (1) REGULAR REPORTS.—
        (A) IN GENERAL.—Regular reports of the Oversight Panel shall include the following:
            (i) The use by the Secretary of authority under this Act, including with respect to the use of contracting authority and administration of the program.

(ii) The impact of purchases made under the Act on the financial markets and financial institutions.

(iii) The extent to which the information made available on transactions under the program has contributed to market transparency.

(iv) The effectiveness of foreclosure mitigation efforts, and the effectiveness of the program from the standpoint of minimizing long-term costs to the taxpayers and maximizing the benefits for taxpayers.

(B) TIMING.—The reports required under this paragraph shall be submitted not later than 30 days after the first exercise by the Secretary of the authority under section 101(a) or 102, and every 30 days thereafter.

(2) SPECIAL REPORT ON REGULATORY REFORM.—The Oversight Panel shall submit a special report on regulatory reform not later than January 20, 2009, analyzing the current state of the regulatory system and its effectiveness at overseeing the participants in the financial system and protecting consumers, and providing recommendations for improvement, including recommendations regarding whether any participants in the financial markets that are currently outside the regulatory system should become subject to the regulatory system, the rationale underlying such recommendation, and whether there are any gaps in existing consumer protections.

(c) MEMBERSHIP.—

(1) IN GENERAL.—The Oversight Panel shall consist of 5 members, as follows:

(A) 1 member appointed by the Speaker of the House of Representatives.

(B) 1 member appointed by the minority leader of the House of Representatives.

(C) 1 member appointed by the majority leader of the Senate.

(D) 1 member appointed by the minority leader of the Senate.

(E) 1 member appointed by the Speaker of the House of Representatives and the majority leader of the Senate, after consultation with the minority leader of the Senate and the minority leader of the House of Representatives.

(2) PAY.—Each member of the Oversight Panel shall each be paid at a rate equal to the daily equivalent of the annual rate of basic pay for level I of the Executive Schedule for each day (including travel time) during which such member is engaged in the actual performance of duties vested in the Commission.

(3) PROHIBITION OF COMPENSATION OF FEDERAL EMPLOYEES.—Members of the Oversight Panel who are full-time officers or employees of the United States or Members of Congress may not receive additional pay, allowances, or benefits by reason of their service on the Oversight Panel.

(4) TRAVEL EXPENSES.—Each member shall receive travel expenses, including per diem in lieu of subsistence, in accordance with applicable provisions under subchapter I of chapter 57 of title 5, United States Code.

(5) QUORUM.—Four members of the Oversight Panel shall constitute a quorum but a lesser number may hold hearings.

(6) VACANCIES.—A vacancy on the Oversight Panel shall be filled in the manner in which the original appointment was made.

(7) MEETINGS.—The Oversight Panel shall meet at the call of the Chairperson or a majority of its members.

(d) STAFF.—

(1) IN GENERAL.—The Oversight Panel may appoint and fix the pay of any personnel as the Commission considers appropriate.

(2) EXPERTS AND CONSULTANTS.—The Oversight Panel may procure temporary and intermittent services under section 3109(b) of title 5, United States Code.

(3) STAFF OF AGENCIES.—Upon request of the Oversight Panel, the head of any Federal department or agency may detail, on a reimbursable basis, any of the personnel of that department or agency to the Oversight Panel to assist it in carrying out its duties under this Act.

(e) POWERS.—

(1) HEARINGS AND SESSIONS.—The Oversight Panel may, for the purpose of carrying out this section, hold hearings, sit and act at times and places, take testimony, and receive evidence as the Panel considers appropriate and may administer oaths or affirmations to witnesses appearing before it.

(2) POWERS OF MEMBERS AND AGENTS.—Any member or agent of the Oversight Panel may, if authorized by the Oversight Panel, take any action which the Oversight Panel is authorized to take by this section.

(3) OBTAINING OFFICIAL DATA.—The Oversight Panel may secure directly from any department or agency of the United States information necessary to enable it to carry out this section. Upon request of the Chairperson of the Oversight Panel, the head of that department or agency shall furnish that information to the Oversight Panel.

(4) REPORTS.—The Oversight Panel shall receive and consider all reports required to be submitted to the Oversight Panel under this Act.

(f) TERMINATION.—The Oversight Panel shall terminate 6 months after the termination date specified in section 120.

(g) FUNDING FOR EXPENSES.—

(1) AUTHORIZATION OF APPROPRIATIONS.— There is authorized to be appropriated to the Oversight Panel such sums as may be necessary for any fiscal year, half of which shall be derived from the applicable account of the House of Representatives, and half of which shall be derived from the contingent fund of the Senate.

(2) REIMBURSEMENT OF AMOUNTS.—An amount equal to the expenses of the Oversight Panel shall be promptly transferred by the Secretary, from time to time upon the presentment of a statement of such expenses by the Chairperson of the Oversight Panel, from funds made available to the Secretary under this Act to the applicable fund of the House of Representatives and the contingent fund of the Senate, as appropriate, as reimbursement for amounts expended from such account and fund under paragraph (1).

SEC. 126. FDIC AUTHORITY.

(a) IN GENERAL.—Section 18(a) of the Federal Deposit Insurance Act (12 U.S.C. 1828(a)) is amended by adding at the end the following new paragraph:

"(4) FALSE ADVERTISING, MISUSE OF FDIC NAMES, AND MISREPRESENTATION TO INDICATE INSURED STATUS.—

"(A) PROHIBITION ON FALSE ADVERTISING AND MISUSE OF FDIC NAMES.—No person may represent or imply that any deposit liability, obligation, certificate, or share is insured or guaranteed by the Corporation, if such deposit liability, obligation, certificate, or share is not insured or guaranteed by the Corporation—

"(i) by using the terms 'Federal Deposit', 'Federal Deposit Insurance', 'Federal Deposit Insurance Corporation', any combination of such terms, or the abbreviation 'FDIC' as part of the business name or firm name of any person, including any corporation, partnership, business trust, association, or other business entity; or

"(ii) by using such terms or any other terms, sign, or symbol as part of an advertisement, solicitation, or other document.

"(B) PROHIBITION ON MISREPRESENTATIONS OF INSURED STATUS.— No person may knowingly misrepresent—

"(i) that any deposit liability, obligation, certificate, or share is insured, under this Act, if such deposit liability, obligation, certificate, or share is not so insured; or

"(ii) the extent to which or the manner in which any deposit liability, obligation, certificate, or share is insured under this Act, if such deposit liability, obligation, certificate, or share is not so insured, to the extent or in the manner represented.

"(C) AUTHORITY OF THE APPROPRIATE FEDERAL BANKING AGENCY.— The appropriate Federal banking agency shall have enforcement authority in the case of a violation of this paragraph by any person for which the agency is the appropriate Federal banking agency, or any institution-affiliated party thereof.

"(D) CORPORATION AUTHORITY IF THE APPROPRIATE FEDERAL BANKING AGENCY FAILS TO FOLLOW RECOMMENDATION.—

"(i) RECOMMENDATION.—The Corporation may recommend in writing to the appropriate Federal banking agency that the agency take any enforcement action authorized under section 8 for purposes of enforcement of this paragraph with respect to any person for which the agency is the appropriate Federal banking agency or any institution-affiliated party thereof.

"(ii) AGENCY RESPONSE.—If the appropriate Federal banking agency does not, within 30 days of the date of receipt of a recommendation under clause (i), take the enforcement action with respect to this paragraph recommended by the Corporation or provide a plan acceptable to the Corporation for responding to the situation presented, the Corporation may take the recommended enforcement action against such person or institution-affiliated party.

"(E) ADDITIONAL AUTHORITY.—In addition to its authority under subparagraphs (C) and (D), for purposes of this paragraph, the Corporation shall have, in the same manner and to the same extent as with respect to a State nonmember insured bank—

"(i) jurisdiction over—

"(I) any person other than a person for which another agency is the appropriate Federal banking agency or any institution-affiliated party thereof; and

"(II) any person that aids or abets a violation of this paragraph by a person described in subclause (I); and

"(ii) for purposes of enforcing the requirements of this paragraph, the authority of the Corporation under—

"(I) section 10(c) to conduct investigations; and

"(II) subsections (b), (c), (d) and (i) of section 8 to conduct enforcement actions.

"(F) OTHER ACTIONS PRESERVED.—No provision of this paragraph shall be construed as barring any action otherwise available, under the laws of the United States or any State, to any Federal or State agency or individual.".

(b) Enforcement Orders.—Section 8(c) of the Federal Deposit Insurance Act (12 U.S.C. 1818(c)) is amended by adding at the end the following new paragraph:

"(4) False advertising or misuse of names to indicate insured status.—

"(A) Temporary order.—

"(i) In general.—If a notice of charges served under subsection (b)(1) specifies on the basis of particular facts that any person engaged or is engaging in conduct described in section 18(a)(4), the Corporation or other appropriate Federal banking agency may issue a temporary order requiring—

"(I) the immediate cessation of any activity or practice described, which gave rise to the notice of charges; and

"(II) affirmative action to prevent any further, or to remedy any existing, violation.

"(ii) Effect of order.—Any temporary order issued under this subparagraph shall take effect upon service.

"(B) Effective period of temporary order.—A temporary order issued under subparagraph (A) shall remain effective and enforceable, pending the completion of an administrative proceeding pursuant to subsection (b)(1) in connection with the notice of charges—

"(i) until such time as the Corporation or other appropriate Federal banking agency dismisses the charges specified in such notice; or

"(ii) if a cease-and-desist order is issued against such person, until the effective date of such order.

"(C) Civil money penalties.—Any violation of section 18(a)(4) shall be subject to civil money penalties, as set forth in subsection (i), except that for any person other than an insured depository institution or an institution-affiliated party that is found to have violated this paragraph, the Corporation or other appropriate Federal banking agency shall not be required to demonstrate any loss to an insured depository institution.".

(c) Unenforceability of Certain Agreements.—Section 13(c) of the Federal Deposit Insurance Act (12 U.S.C. 1823(c)) is amended by adding at the end the following new paragraph:

"(11) Unenforceability of certain agreements.—No provision contained in any existing or future standstill, confidentiality, or other agreement that, directly or indirectly—

"(A) affects, restricts, or limits the ability of any person to offer to acquire or acquire,

"(B) prohibits any person from offering to acquire or acquiring, or

"(C) prohibits any person from using any previously disclosed information in connection with any such offer to acquire or acquisition of, all or part of any insured depository institution, including any liabilities, assets, or interest therein, in connection with any transaction in which the Corporation exercises its authority under section 11 or 13, shall be enforceable against or impose any liability on such person, as such enforcement or liability shall be contrary to public policy.".

(d) TECHNICAL AND CONFORMING AMENDMENTS.—Section 18 of the Federal Deposit Insurance Act (12 U.S.C. 1828) is amended—

(1) in subsection (a)(3)—

(A) by striking "this subsection" the first place that term appears and inserting "paragraph (1)"; and

(B) by striking "this subsection" the second place that term appears and inserting "paragraph (2)"; and

(2) in the heading for subsection (a), by striking "INSURANCE LOGO.—" and inserting "REPRESENTATIONS OF DEPOSIT INSURANCE.—".

SEC. 127. COOPERATION WITH THE FBI.

Any Federal financial regulatory agency shall cooperate with the Federal Bureau of Investigation and other law enforcement agencies investigating fraud, misrepresentation, and malfeasance with respect to development, advertising, and sale of financial products.

SEC. 128. ACCELERATION OF EFFECTIVE DATE.

Section 203 of the Financial Services Regulatory Relief Act of 2006 (12 U.S.C. 461 note) is amended by striking "October 1, 2011" and inserting "October 1, 2008".

SEC. 129. DISCLOSURES ON EXERCISE OF LOAN AUTHORITY.

(a) IN GENERAL.—Not later than 7 days after the date on which the Board exercises its authority under the third paragraph of section 13 of the Federal Reserve Act (12 U.S.C. 343; relating to discounts for individuals, partnerships, and corporations) the Board shall provide to the Committee on Banking, Housing, and Urban Affairs of the Senate and the Committee on Financial Services of the House of Representatives a report which includes—

(1) the justification for exercising the authority; and

(2) the specific terms of the actions of the Board, including the size and duration of the lending, available information concerning the value of any collateral held with respect to such a loan, the recipient of warrants or any other potential equity in exchange for the loan, and any expected cost to the taxpayers for such exercise.

(b) PERIODIC UPDATES.—The Board shall provide updates to the Committees specified in subsection (a) not less frequently than once every 60 days while the subject loan is outstanding, including—

(1) the status of the loan;

(2) the value of the collateral held by the Federal reserve bank which initiated the loan; and

(3) the projected cost to the taxpayers of the loan.

(c) CONFIDENTIALITY.—The information submitted to the Congress under this section may be kept confidential, upon the written request of the Chairman of the Board, in which case it shall made available only to the Chairpersons and Ranking Members of the Committees described in subsection (a).

(d) APPLICABILITY.—The provisions of this section shall be in force for all uses of the authority provided under section 13 of the Federal Reserve Act occurring during the period beginning on March 1, 2008 and ending on the after the date of enactment of this Act, and reports described in subsection (a) shall be required beginning not later than 30 days after that date of enactment, with respect to any such exercise of authority.

(e) SHARING OF INFORMATION.—Any reports required under this section shall also be submitted to the Congressional Oversight Panel established under section 125.

SEC. 130. TECHNICAL CORRECTIONS.

(a) IN GENERAL.—Section 128(b)(2) of the Truth in Lending Act (15 U.S.C. 1638(b)(2)), as amended by section 2502 of the Mortgage Disclosure Improvement Act of 2008 (Public Law 110-289), is amended—

(1) in subparagraph (A), by striking "In the case" and inserting "Except as provided in subpara-graph (G), in the case"; and

(2) by amending subparagraph (G) to read as follows:

"(G)(i) In the case of an extension of credit relating to a plan described in section 101(53D) of title 11, United States Code—

"(I) the requirements of subparagraphs (A) through (E) shall not apply; and

"(II) a good faith estimate of the disclosures required under subsection (a) shall be made in accordance with regulations of the Board under section 121(c) before such credit is extended, or shall be delivered or placed in the mail not later than 3 business days after the date on which the creditor receives the written application of the consumer for such credit, whichever is earlier.

"(ii) If a disclosure statement furnished within 3 business days of the written application (as provided under clause (i)(II)) contains an annual percentage rate which is subsequently rendered inaccurate, within the meaning of section 107(c), the creditor shall furnish another disclosure statement at the time of settlement or consummation of the transaction.".

(b) EFFECTIVE DATE.—The amendments made by subsection (a) shall take effect as if included in the amendments made by section 2502 of the Mortgage Disclosure Improvement Act of 2008 (Public Law 110-289).

SEC. 131. EXCHANGE STABILIZATION FUND REIMBURSEMENT.

(a) REIMBURSEMENT.—The Secretary shall reimburse the Exchange Stabilization Fund established under section 5302 of title 31, United States Code, for any funds that are used for the Treasury Money Market Funds Guaranty Program for the United States money market mutual fund industry, from funds under this Act.

(b) LIMITS ON USE OF EXCHANGE STABILIZATION FUND.—The Secretary is prohibited from using the Exchange Stabilization Fund for the establishment of any future guaranty programs for the United States money market mutual fund industry.

SEC. 132. AUTHORITY TO SUSPEND MARK-TO-MARKET ACCOUNTING.

(a) AUTHORITY.—The Securities and Exchange Commission shall have the authority under the securities laws (as such term is defined in section 3(a)(47) of the Securities Exchange Act of 1934 (15 U.S.C. 78c(a)(47)) to suspend, by rule, regulation, or order, the application of Statement Number 157 of the Financial Accounting Standards Board for any issuer (as such term is defined in section 3(a)(8) of such Act) or with respect to any class or category of transaction if the Commission determines that is necessary or appropriate in the public interest and is consistent with the protection of investors.

(b) SAVINGS PROVISION.—Nothing in subsection (a) shall be construed to restrict or limit any authority of the Securities and Exchange Commission under securities laws as in effect on the date of enactment of this Act.

SEC. 133. STUDY ON MARK-TO-MARKET ACCOUNTING.

(a) STUDY.—The Securities and Exchange Commission, in consultation with the Board and the Secretary, shall conduct a study on mark-to-market accounting standards as provided in Statement Number 157 of the Financial Accounting Standards Board, as such standards are applicable to financial institutions, including depository institutions. Such a study shall consider at a minimum—

(1) the effects of such accounting standards on a financial institution's balance sheet;

(2) the impacts of such accounting on bank failures in 2008;

(3) the impact of such standards on the quality of financial information available to investors;

(4) the process used by the Financial Accounting Standards Board in developing accounting standards;

(5) the advisability and feasibility of modifications to such standards; and

(6) alternative accounting standards to those provided in such Statement Number 157.

(b) REPORT.—The Securities and Exchange Commission shall submit to Congress a report of such study before the end of the 90-day period beginning on the date of the enactment of this Act containing the findings and determinations of the Commission, including such administrative and legislative recommendations as the Commission determines appropriate.

SEC. 134. RECOUPMENT.

Upon the expiration of the 5-year period beginning upon the date of the enactment of this Act, the Director of the Office of Management and Budget, in consultation with the Director of the Congressional Budget Office, shall submit a report to the Congress on the net amount within the Troubled Asset Relief Program under this Act. In any case where there is a shortfall, the President shall submit a legislative proposal that recoups from the financial industry an amount equal to the shortfall in order to ensure that the Troubled Asset Relief Program does not add to the deficit or national debt.

SEC. 135. PRESERVATION OF AUTHORITY.

With the exception of section 131, nothing in this Act may be construed to limit the authority of the Secretary or the Board under any other provision of law.

SEC. 136. TEMPORARY INCREASE IN DEPOSIT AND SHARE INSURANCE COVERAGE.

(a) FEDERAL DEPOSIT INSURANCE ACT; TEMPORARY INCREASE IN DEPOSIT INSURANCE.—

(1) INCREASED AMOUNT.—Effective only during the period beginning on the date of enactment of this Act and ending on December 31, 2009, section 11(a)(1)(E) of the Federal Deposit Insurance Act (12 U.S.C. 1821(a)(1)(E)) shall apply with "$250,000" substituted for "$100,000".

(2) TEMPORARY INCREASE NOT TO BE CONSIDERED FOR SETTING ASSESSMENTS.—The temporary increase in the standard maximum deposit insurance amount made under paragraph (1) shall not be taken into account by the Board of Directors of the Corporation for purposes of setting assessments under section 7(b)(2) of the Federal Deposit Insurance Act (12 U.S.C. 1817(b)(2)).

(3) BORROWING LIMITS TEMPORARILY LIFTED.—During the period beginning on the date of enactment of this Act and ending on December 31, 2009, the Board of Directors of the Corporation may request from the Secretary, and the Secretary shall approve, a loan or loans in an amount or amounts necessary to carry out this subsection, without regard to the limitations on such borrowing under section 14(a) and 15(c) of the Federal Deposit Insurance Act (12 U.S.C. 1824(a), 1825(c)).

(b) FEDERAL CREDIT UNION ACT; TEMPORARY INCREASE IN SHARE INSURANCE.—

(1) INCREASED AMOUNT.—Effective only during the period beginning on the date of enactment of this Act and ending on December 31, 2009, section 207(k)(5) of the Federal Credit Union Act (12 U.S.C. 1787(k)(5)) shall apply with "$250,000" substituted for "$100,000".

(2) TEMPORARY INCREASE NOT TO BE CONSIDERED FOR SETTING INSURANCE PREMIUM CHARGES.—The temporary increase in the standard maximum share insurance amount made under paragraph (1) shall not be taken into account by the National Credit Union Administration Board for purposes of setting insurance premium charges under section 202(c)(2) of the Federal Credit Union Act (12 U.S.C. 1782(c)(2)).

(3) BORROWING LIMITS TEMPORARILY LIFTED.—During the period beginning on the date of enactment of this Act and ending on December 31, 2009, the National Credit Union Administration Board may request from the Secretary, and the Secretary shall approve, a loan or loans in an amount or amounts necessary to carry out this subsection, without regard to the limitations on such borrowing under section 203(d)(1) of the Federal Credit Union Act (12 U.S.C. 1783(d)(1)).

(c) NOT FOR USE IN INFLATION ADJUSTMENTS.—The temporary increase in the standard maximum deposit insurance amount made under this section shall not be used to make any inflation adjustment under section 11(a)(1)(F) of the Federal Deposit Insurance Act (12 U.S.C. 1821(a)(1)(F)) for purposes of that Act or the Federal Credit Union Act.

TITLE II—BUDGET-RELATED PROVISIONS

SEC. 201. INFORMATION FOR CONGRESSIONAL SUPPORT AGENCIES.

Upon request, and to the extent otherwise consistent with law, all information used by the Secretary in connection with activities authorized under this Act (including the records to which the Comptroller General is entitled under this Act) shall be made available to congressional support agencies (in accordance with their obligations to support the Congress as set out in their authorizing statutes) for the purposes of assisting the committees of Congress with conducting oversight, monitoring, and analysis of the activities authorized under this Act.

SEC. 202. REPORTS BY THE OFFICE OF MANAGEMENT AND BUDGET AND THE CONGRESSIONAL BUDGET OFFICE.

(a) REPORTS BY THE OFFICE OF MANAGEMENT AND BUDGET.—Within 60 days of the first exercise of the authority granted in section 101(a), but in no case later than December 31, 2008, and semiannually thereafter, the Office of Management and Budget shall report to the President and the Congress—

(1) the estimate, notwithstanding section 502(5)(F) of the Federal Credit Reform Act of 1990 (2 U.S.C. 661a(5)(F)), as of the first business day that is at least 30 days prior to the issuance of the report, of the cost of the troubled assets, and guarantees of the troubled assets, determined in accordance with section 123;

(2) the information used to derive the estimate, including assets purchased or guaranteed, prices paid, revenues received, the impact on the deficit and debt, and a description of any outstanding commitments to purchase troubled assets; and

(3) a detailed analysis of how the estimate has changed from the previous report.

Beginning with the second report under subsection (a), the Office of Management and Budget shall explain the differences between the Congressional Budget Office estimates delivered in accordance with subsection (b) and prior Office of Management and Budget estimates.

(b) REPORTS BY THE CONGRESSIONAL BUDGET OFFICE.—Within 45 days of receipt by the Congress of each report from the Office of Management and Budget under subsection (a), the Congressional Budget Office shall report to the Congress the Congressional Budget Office's assessment of the report submitted by the Office of Management and Budget, including—

    (1) the cost of the troubled assets and guarantees of the troubled assets,

    (2) the information and valuation methods used to calculate such cost, and

    (3) the impact on the deficit and the debt.

(c) FINANCIAL EXPERTISE.—In carrying out the duties in this subsection or performing analyses of activities under this Act, the Director of the Congressional Budget Office may employ personnel and procure the services of experts and consultants.

(d) AUTHORIZATION OF APPROPRIATIONS.—There are authorized to be appropriated such sums as may be necessary to produce reports required by this section.

SEC. 203. ANALYSIS IN PRESIDENT'S BUDGET.

(a) IN GENERAL.—Section 1105(a) of title 31, United States Code, is amended by adding at the end the following new paragraph:

"(35) as supplementary materials, a separate analysis of the budgetary effects for all prior fiscal years, the current fiscal year, the fiscal year for which the budget is submitted, and ensuing fiscal years of the actions the Secretary of the Treasury has taken or plans to take using any authority provided in the Emergency Economic Stabilization Act of 2008, including—

"(A) an estimate of the current value of all assets purchased, sold, and guaranteed under the authority provided in the Emergency Economic Stabilization Act of 2008 using methodology required by the Federal Credit Reform Act of 1990 (2 U.S.C. 661 et seq.) and section 123 of the Emergency Economic Stabilization Act of 2008;

"(B) an estimate of the deficit, the debt held by the public, and the gross Federal debt using methodology required by the Federal Credit Reform Act of 1990 and section 123 of the Emergency Economic Stabilization Act of 2008;

"(C) an estimate of the current value of all assets purchased, sold, and guaranteed under the authority provided in the Emergency Economic Stabilization Act of 2008 calculated on a cash basis;

"(D) a revised estimate of the deficit, the debt held by the public, and the gross Federal debt, substituting the cash-based estimates in subparagraph (C) for the estimates calculated under subparagraph (A) pursuant to the Federal Credit Reform Act of 1990 and section 123 of the Emergency Economic Stabilization Act of 2008; and

"(E) the portion of the deficit which can be attributed to any action taken by the Secretary using authority provided by the Emergency Economic Stabilization Act of 2008 and the extent to which the change in the deficit since the most recent estimate is due to a re-estimate using the methodology required by the Federal Credit Reform Act of 1990 and section 123 of the Emergency Economic Stabilization Act of 2008."

(b) CONSULTATION.—In implementing this section, the Director of Office of Management and Budget shall consult periodically, but at least annually, with the Committee on the Budget of the House of Representatives, the Committee on the Budget of the Senate, and the Director of the Congressional Budget Office.

(c) EFFECTIVE DATE.—This section and the amendment made by this section shall apply beginning with respect to the fiscal year 2010 budget submission of the President.

SEC. 204. EMERGENCY TREATMENT.

All provisions of this Act are designated as an emergency requirement and necessary to meet emergency needs pursuant to section 204(a) of S. Con. Res 21 (110th Congress), the concurrent resolution on the budget for fiscal year 2008 and rescissions of any amounts provided in this Act shall not be counted for purposes of budget enforcement.

TITLE III—TAX PROVISIONS

SEC. 301. GAIN OR LOSS FROM SALE OR EXCHANGE OF CERTAIN PREFERRED STOCK.

(a) IN GENERAL.—For purposes of the Internal Revenue Code of 1986, gain or loss from the sale or exchange of any applicable preferred stock by any applicable financial institution shall be treated as ordinary income or loss.

(b) APPLICABLE PREFERRED STOCK.—For purposes of this section, the term "applicable preferred stock" means any stock—

(1) which is preferred stock in—

(A) the Federal National Mortgage Association, established pursuant to the Federal National Mortgage Association Charter Act (12 U.S.C. 1716 et seq.), or

    (B) the Federal Home Loan Mortgage Corporation, established pursuant to the Federal Home Loan Mortgage Corporation Act (12 U.S.C. 1451 et seq.), and

    (2) which—

        (A) was held by the applicable financial institution on September 6, 2008, or

        (B) was sold or exchanged by the applicable financial institution on or after January 1, 2008, and before September 7, 2008.

(c) APPLICABLE FINANCIAL INSTITUTION.—For purposes of this section:

    (1) IN GENERAL.—Except as provided in paragraph (2), the term "applicable financial institution" means—

        (A) a financial institution referred to in section 582(c)(2) of the Internal Revenue Code of 1986, or

        (B) a depository institution holding company (as defined in section 3(w)(1) of the Federal Deposit Insurance Act (12 U.S.C. 1813(w)(1))).

    (2) SPECIAL RULES FOR CERTAIN SALES.—In the case of—

        (A) a sale or exchange described in subsection (b)(2)(B), an entity shall be treated as an applicable financial institution only if it was an entity described in subparagraph (A) or (B) of paragraph (1) at the time of the sale or exchange, and

        (B) a sale or exchange after September 6, 2008, of preferred stock described in subsection (b)(2)(A), an entity shall be treated as an applicable financial institution only if it was an entity described in subparagraph (A) or (B) of paragraph (1) at all times during the period beginning on September 6, 2008, and ending on the date of the sale or exchange of the preferred stock.

(d) SPECIAL RULE FOR CERTAIN PROPERTY NOT HELD ON SEPTEMBER 6, 2008.—The Secretary of the Treasury or the Secretary's delegate may extend the application of this section to all or a portion of the gain or loss from a sale or exchange in any case where—

    (1) an applicable financial institution sells or exchanges applicable preferred stock after September 6, 2008, which the applicable financial institution did not hold on such date, but the basis of which in the hands of the applicable financial institution at the time of the sale or exchange is the same as the basis in the hands of the person which held such stock on such date, or

    (2) the applicable financial institution is a partner in a partnership which—

        (A) held such stock on September 6, 2008, and later sold or exchanged such stock, or

        (B) sold or exchanged such stock during the period described in subsection (b)(2)(B).

(e) REGULATORY AUTHORITY.—The Secretary of the Treasury or the Secretary's delegate may prescribe such guidance, rules, or regulations as are necessary to carry out the purposes of this section.

(f) EFFECTIVE DATE.—This section shall apply to sales or exchanges occurring after December 31, 2007, in taxable years ending after such date.

SEC. 302. SPECIAL RULES FOR TAX TREATMENT OF EXECUTIVE COMPENSATION OF EMPLOYERS PARTICIPATING IN THE TROUBLED ASSETS RELIEF PROGRAM.

(a) DENIAL OF DEDUCTION.—Subsection (m) of section 162 of the Internal Revenue Code of 1986 is amended by adding at the end the following new paragraph:

"(5) SPECIAL RULE FOR APPLICATION TO EMPLOYERS PARTICIPATING IN THE TROUBLED ASSETS RELIEF PROGRAM.—

"(A) IN GENERAL.—In the case of an applicable employer, no deduction shall be allowed under this chapter—

"(i) in the case of executive remuneration for any applicable taxable year which is attributable to services performed by a covered executive during such applicable taxable year, to the extent that the amount of such remuneration exceeds $500,000, or

"(ii) in the case of deferred deduction executive remuneration for any taxable year for services performed during any applicable taxable year by a covered executive, to the extent that the amount of such remuneration exceeds $500,000 reduced (but not below zero) by the sum of—

"(I) the executive remuneration for such applicable taxable year, plus

"(II) the portion of the deferred deduction executive remuneration for such services which was taken into account under this clause in a preceding taxable year.

"(B) APPLICABLE EMPLOYER.—For purposes of this paragraph—

"(i) IN GENERAL.—Except as provided in clause (ii), the term 'applicable employer' means any employer from whom 1 or more troubled assets are acquired under a program established by the Secretary under section 101(a) of the Emergency Economic Stabilization Act of 2008 if the aggregate amount of the assets so acquired for all taxable years exceeds $300,000,000.

"(ii) DISREGARD OF CERTAIN ASSETS SOLD THROUGH DIRECT PURCHASE.—If the only sales of troubled assets by an employer under the program described in clause (i) are through 1 or more direct purchases (within the meaning of section 113(c) of the Emergency Economic Stabilization Act of 2008), such assets shall not be taken into account under clause (i) in determining whether the employer is an applicable employer for purposes of this paragraph.

"(iii) AGGREGATION RULES.—Two or more persons who are treated as a single employer under subsection (b) or (c) of section 414 shall be treated as a single employer, except that in applying section 1563(a) for purposes of either such subsection, paragraphs (2) and (3) thereof shall be disregarded.

"(C) APPLICABLE TAXABLE YEAR.—For purposes of this paragraph, the term 'applicable taxable year' means, with respect to any employer—

"(i) the first taxable year of the employer—

"(I) which includes any portion of the period during which the authorities under section 101(a) of the Emergency Economic Stabilization Act of 2008 are in effect (determined under section 120 thereof), and

"(II) in which the aggregate amount of troubled assets acquired from the employer during the taxable year pursuant to such authorities (other than assets to which subparagraph (B)(ii) applies), when added to the aggregate amount so acquired for all preceding taxable years, exceeds $300,000,000, and

"(ii) any subsequent taxable year which includes any portion of such period.

(D) COVERED EXECUTIVE.—For purposes of this paragraph—

"(i) IN GENERAL.—The term 'covered executive' means, with respect to any applicable taxable year, any employee—

"(I) who, at any time during the portion of the taxable year during which the authorities under section 101(a) of the Emergency Economic Stabilization Act of 2008 are in effect (determined under section 120 thereof), is the chief executive officer of the applicable employer or the chief financial officer of the applicable employer, or an individual acting in either such capacity, or

"(II) who is described in clause (ii).

"(ii) HIGHEST COMPENSATED EMPLOYEES.—An employee is described in this clause if the employee is 1 of the 3 highest compensated officers of the applicable employer for the taxable year (other than an individual described in clause (i)(I)), determined—

"(I) on the basis of the shareholder disclosure rules for compensation under the Securities Exchange Act of

1934 (without regard to whether those rules apply to the employer), and

"(II) by only taking into account employees employed during the portion of the taxable year described in clause (i)(I).

"(iii) EMPLOYEE REMAINS COVERED EXECUTIVE.—If an employee is a covered executive with respect to an applicable employer for any applicable taxable year, such employee shall be treated as a covered executive with respect to such employer for all subsequent applicable taxable years and for all subsequent taxable years in which deferred deduction executive remuneration with respect to services performed in all such applicable taxable years would (but for this paragraph) be deductible.

"(E) EXECUTIVE REMUNERATION.—For purposes of this paragraph, the term 'executive remuneration' means the applicable employee remuneration of the covered executive, as determined under paragraph (4) without regard to subparagraphs (B), (C), and (D) thereof. Such term shall not include any deferred deduction executive remuneration with respect to services performed in a prior applicable taxable year.

"(F) DEFERRED DEDUCTION EXECUTIVE REMUNERATION.—For purposes of this paragraph, the term 'deferred deduction executive remuneration' means remuneration which would be executive remuneration for services performed in an applicable taxable year but for the fact that the deduction under this chapter (determined without regard to this paragraph) for such remuneration is allowable in a subsequent taxable year.

"(G) COORDINATION.—Rules similar to the rules of subparagraphs (F) and (G) of paragraph (4) shall apply for purposes of this paragraph.

"(H) REGULATORY AUTHORITY.—The Secretary may prescribe such guidance, rules, or regulations as are necessary to carry out the purposes of this paragraph and the Emergency Economic Stabilization Act of 2008, including the extent to which this paragraph applies in the case of any acquisition, merger, or reorganization of an applicable employer.".

(b) GOLDEN PARACHUTE RULE.—Section 280G of the Internal Revenue Code of 1986 is amended—

(1) by redesignating subsection (e) as subsection (f), and

(2) by inserting after subsection (d) the following new subsection:

"(e) SPECIAL RULE FOR APPLICATION TO EMPLOYERS PARTICIPATING IN THE TROUBLED ASSETS RELIEF PROGRAM.—

"(1) IN GENERAL.—In the case of the severance from employment of a covered executive of an applicable employer during the period during which the authorities under section 101(a) of the Emergency Economic Stabilization Act of 2008 are in effect (determined under section 120 of such Act), this section shall be applied to payments to such executive with the following modifications:

"(A) Any reference to a disqualified individual (other than in subsection (c)) shall be treated as a reference to a covered executive.

"(B) Any reference to a change described in subsection (b)(2)(A)(i) shall be treated as a reference to an applicable severance from employment of a covered executive, and any reference to a payment contingent on such a change shall be treated as a reference to any payment made during an applicable taxable year of the employer on account of such applicable severance from employment.

"(C) Any reference to a corporation shall be treated as a reference to an applicable employer.

"(D) The provisions of subsections (b)(2)(C), (b)(4), (b)(5), and (d)(5) shall not apply.

(2) DEFINITIONS AND SPECIAL RULES.—For purposes of this subsection:

"(A) DEFINITIONS.—Any term used in this subsection which is also used in section 162(m)(5) shall have the meaning given such term by such section.

"(B) APPLICABLE SEVERANCE FROM EMPLOYMENT.—The term 'applicable severance from employment' means any severance from employment of a covered executive—

"(i) by reason of an involuntary termination of the executive by the employer, or

"(ii) in connection with any bankruptcy, liquidation, or receivership of the employer.

"(C) COORDINATION AND OTHER RULES.—

"(i) IN GENERAL.—If a payment which is treated as a parachute payment by reason of this subsection is also a parachute payment determined without regard to this subsection, this subsection shall not apply to such payment.

"(ii) REGULATORY AUTHORITY.—The Secretary may prescribe such guidance, rules, or regulations as are necessary—

"(I) to carry out the purposes of this subsection and the Emergency Economic Stabilization Act of 2008, including the extent to which this subsection applies in the case of any acquisition, merger, or reorganization of an applicable employer,

"(II) to apply this section and section 4999 in cases where one or more payments with respect to any individual are treated as parachute payments by reason of this subsection, and other payments with respect to such individual are treated as parachute payments under this section without regard to this subsection, and

"(III) to prevent the avoidance of the application of this section through the mischaracterization of a severance from employment as other than an applicable severance from employment.".

(c) EFFECTIVE DATES.—

(1) IN GENERAL.—The amendment made by subsection (a) shall apply to taxable years ending on or after the date of the enactment of this Act.

(2) GOLDEN PARACHUTE RULE.—The amendments made by subsection (b) shall apply to payments with respect to severances occurring during the period during which the authorities under section 101(a) of this Act are in effect (determined under section 120 of this Act).

SEC. 303. EXTENSION OF EXCLUSION OF INCOME FROM DISCHARGE OF QUALIFIED PRINCIPAL RESIDENCE INDEBTEDNESS.

(a) EXTENSION.—Subparagraph (E) of section 108(a)(1) of the Internal Revenue Code of 1986 is amended by striking "January 1, 2010" and inserting "January 1, 2013".

(b) EFFECTIVE DATE.—The amendment made by this section shall apply to discharges of indebtedness oc curring on or after January 1, 2010.

DIVISION B—ENERGY IMPROVEMENT AND EXTENSION ACT OF 2008

SECTION 1. SHORT TITLE, ETC.

(a) SHORT TITLE.—This division may be cited as the "Energy Improvement and Extension Act of 2008".

(b) REFERENCE.—Except as otherwise expressly provided, whenever in this division an amendment or repeal is expressed in terms of an amendment to, or repeal of, a section or other provision, the reference shall be considered to be made to a section or other provision of the Internal Revenue Code of 1986.

(c) TABLE OF CONTENTS.—The table of contents for this division is as follows:

Excerpts from the Emergency Economic Stabilization Act

Sec. 1. Short title, etc.

TITLE I—ENERGY PRODUCTION INCENTIVES
Subtitle A—Renewable Energy Incentives
Sec. 101. Renewable energy credit.
Sec. 102. Production credit for electricity produced from marine renewables.
Sec. 103. Energy credit.
Sec. 104. Energy credit for small wind property.
Sec. 105. Energy credit for geothermal heat pump systems.
Sec. 106. Credit for residential energy efficient property.
Sec. 107. New clean renewable energy bonds.
Sec. 108. Credit for steel industry fuel.
Sec. 109. Special rule to implement FERC and State electric restructuring policy.

Subtitle B—Carbon Mitigation and Coal Provisions
Sec. 111. Expansion and modification of advanced coal project investment credit.
Sec. 112. Expansion and modification of coal gasification investment credit.
Sec. 113. Temporary increase in coal excise tax; funding of Black Lung Disability Trust Fund.
Sec. 114. Special rules for refund of the coal excise tax to certain coal producers and exporters.
Sec. 115. Tax credit for carbon dioxide sequestration.
Sec. 116. Certain income and gains relating to industrial source carbon dioxide treated as qualifying income for publicly traded partnerships.
Sec. 117. Carbon audit of the tax code.

TITLE II—TRANSPORTATION AND DOMESTIC FUEL SECURITY PROVISIONS
Sec. 201. Inclusion of cellulosic biofuel in bonus depreciation for biomass ethanol plant property.
Sec. 202. Credits for biodiesel and renewable diesel.
Sec. 203. Clarification that credits for fuel are designed to provide an incentive for United States production.
Sec. 204. Extension and modification of alternative fuel credit.
Sec. 205. Credit for new qualified plug-in electric drive motor vehicles.
Sec. 206. Exclusion from heavy truck tax for idling reduction units and advanced insulation.
Sec. 207. Alternative fuel vehicle refueling property credit.
Sec. 208. Certain income and gains relating to alcohol fuels and mixtures, bio-diesel fuels and mixtures, and alternative fuels and mixtures treated as qualifying income for publicly traded partnerships.
Sec. 209. Extension and modification of election to expense certain refineries.
Sec. 210. Extension of suspension of taxable income limit on percentage depletion for oil and natural gas produced from marginal properties.
Sec. 211. Transportation fringe benefit to bicycle commuters.

TITLE III—ENERGY CONSERVATION AND EFFICIENCY PROVISIONS
Sec. 301. Qualified energy conservation bonds.
Sec. 302. Credit for nonbusiness energy property.
Sec. 303. Energy efficient commercial buildings deduction.
Sec. 304. New energy efficient home credit.

Sec. 305. Modifications of energy efficient appliance credit for appliances produced after 2007.
Sec. 306. Accelerated recovery period for depreciation of smart meters and smart grid systems.
Sec. 307. Qualified green building and sustainable design projects.
Sec. 308. Special depreciation allowance for certain reuse and recycling property.

TITLE IV—REVENUE PROVISIONS

Sec. 401. Limitation of deduction for income attributable to domestic production of oil, gas, or primary products thereof.
Sec. 402. Elimination of the different treatment of foreign oil and gas extraction income and foreign oil related income for purposes of the foreign tax credit.
Sec. 403. Broker reporting of customer's basis in securities transactions.
Sec. 404. 0.2 percent FUTA surtax.
Sec. 405. Increase and extension of Oil Spill Liability Trust Fund tax.

TITLE I—ENERGY PRODUCTION INCENTIVES

Subtitle A—Renewable Energy Incentives

SEC. 101. RENEWABLE ENERGY CREDIT.

(a) EXTENSION OF CREDIT.—

(1) 1-YEAR EXTENSION FOR WIND AND REFINED COAL FACILITIES.—Paragraphs (1) and (8) of section 45(d) are each amended by striking "January 1, 2009" and inserting "January 1, 2010".

(2) 2-YEAR EXTENSION FOR CERTAIN OTHER FACILITIES.—Each of the following provisions of section 45(d) is amended by striking "January 1, 2009" and inserting "January 1, 2011":

(A) Clauses (i) and (ii) of paragraph (2)(A).

(B) Clauses (i)(I) and (ii) of paragraph (3)(A).

(C) Paragraph (4).

(D) Paragraph (5).

(E) Paragraph (6).

(F) Paragraph (7).

(G) Subparagraphs (A) and (B) of paragraph (9).

(b) MODIFICATION OF REFINED COAL AS A QUALIFIED ENERGY RESOURCE.—

(1) ELIMINATION OF INCREASED MARKET VALUE TEST.—Section 45(c)(7)(A)(i) (defining refined coal), as amended by section 108, is amended—

(A) by striking subclause (IV),

(B) by adding "and" at the end of subclause (II), and

(C) by striking ", and" at the end of subclause (III) and inserting a period.

(2) INCREASE IN REQUIRED EMISSION REDUCTION.—Section 45(c)(7)(B) (defining qualified emission reduction) is amended by inserting "at least 40 percent of the emissions of" after "nitrogen oxide and".

(c) TRASH FACILITY CLARIFICATION.—Paragraph (7) of section 45(d) is amended—

(1) by striking "facility which burns" and inserting "facility (other than a facility described in paragraph (6)) which uses", and

(2) by striking "COMBUSTION".

(d) EXPANSION OF BIOMASS FACILITIES.—

(1) OPEN-LOOP BIOMASS FACILITIES.—Paragraph (3) of section 45(d) is amended by redesignating subparagraph (B) as subparagraph (C) and by inserting after subparagraph (A) the following new subparagraph:

"(B) EXPANSION OF FACILITY.—Such term shall include a new unit placed in service after the date of the enactment of this subparagraph in connection with a facility described in subparagraph (A), but only to the extent of the increased amount of electricity produced at the facility by reason of such new unit.".

(2) CLOSED-LOOP BIOMASS FACILITIES.—Paragraph (2) of section 45(d) is amended by redesignating subparagraph (B) as subparagraph (C) and inserting after subparagraph (A) the following new subparagraph:

"(B) EXPANSION OF FACILITY.—Such term shall include a new unit placed in service after the date of the enactment of this subparagraph in connection with a facility described in subparagraph (A)(i), but only to the extent of the increased amount of electricity produced at the facility by reason of such new unit.".

(e) MODIFICATION OF RULES FOR HYDROPOWER PRODUCTION.—Subparagraph (C) of section 45(c)(8) is amended to read as follows:

"(C) NONHYDROELECTRIC DAM.—For purposes of subparagraph (A), a facility is described in this subparagraph if—

"(i) the hydroelectric project installed on the nonhydroelectric dam is licensed by the Federal Energy Regulatory Commission and meets all other applicable environmental, licensing, and regulatory requirements,

"(ii) the nonhydroelectric dam was placed in service before the date of the enactment of this paragraph and operated for flood control, navigation, or water supply purposes and did not produce hydroelectric power on the date of the enactment of this paragraph, and

"(iii) the hydroelectric project is operated so that the water surface elevation at any given location and time that would have occurred in the absence of the hydroelectric project is maintained, subject to any license requirements imposed under applicable law that change the water surface elevation for the purpose of improving environmental quality of the affected waterway.

The Secretary, in consultation with the Federal Energy Regulatory Commission, shall certify if a hydroelectric project licensed at a nonhydro-electric dam meets the criteria in clause (iii). Nothing in this section shall affect the standards under which the Federal Energy Regulatory Commission issues licenses for and regulates hydropower projects under part I of the Federal Power Act."

(f) EFFECTIVE DATE.—

(1) IN GENERAL.—Except as otherwise pro vided in this subsection, the amendments made by this section shall apply to property originally placed in service after December 31, 2008.

(2) REFINED COAL.—The amendments made by subsection (b) shall apply to coal produced and sold from facilities placed in service after December 31, 2008.

(3) TRASH FACILITY CLARIFICATION.—The amendments made by subsection (c) shall apply to electricity produced and sold after the date of the enactment of this Act.

(4) EXPANSION OF BIOMASS FACILITIES.—The amendments made by subsection (d) shall apply to property placed in service after the date of the enactment of this Act.

SEC. 102. PRODUCTION CREDIT FOR ELECTRICITY PRODUCED FROM MARINE RENEWABLES.

(a) IN GENERAL.—Paragraph (1) of section 45(c) is amended by striking "and" at the end of subparagraph (G), by striking the period at the end of subparagraph (H) and inserting ", and", and by adding at the end the following new subparagraph:

"(I) marine and hydrokinetic renewable energy.".

(b) MARINE RENEWABLES.—Subsection (c) of section 45 is amended by adding at the end the following new paragraph:

"(10) MARINE AND HYDROKINETIC RENEWABLE ENERGY.—

"(A) IN GENERAL.—The term 'marine and hydrokinetic renewable energy' means energy derived from—

"(i) waves, tides, and currents in oceans, estuaries, and tidal areas,

"(ii) free flowing water in rivers, lakes, and streams,

"(iii) free flowing water in an irrigation system, canal, or other man-made channel, including projects that utilize

148

non-mechanical structures to accelerate the flow of water for electric power production purposes, or

"(iv) differentials in ocean temperature (ocean thermal energy conversion).

"(B) EXCEPTIONS.—Such term shall not include any energy which is derived from any source which utilizes a dam, diversionary structure (except as provided in subparagraph (A)(iii)), or impoundment for electric power production purposes."

(c) DEFINITION OF FACILITY.—Subsection (d) of section 45 is amended by adding at the end the following new paragraph:

"(11) MARINE AND HYDROKINETIC RENEWABLE ENERGY FACILITIES.—In the case of a facility producing electricity from marine and hydrokinetic renewable energy, the term 'qualified facility' means any facility owned by the taxpayer—

"(A) which has a nameplate capacity rating of at least 150 kilowatts, and

"(B) which is originally placed in service on or after the date of the enactment of this paragraph and before January 1, 2012."

(d) CREDIT RATE.—Subparagraph (A) of section 45(b)(4) is amended by striking "or (9)" and inserting "(9), or (11)".

(e) COORDINATION WITH SMALL IRRIGATION POWER.—Paragraph (5) of section 45(d), as amended by section 101, is amended by striking "January 1, 2012" and inserting "the date of the enactment of paragraph (11)".

(f) EFFECTIVE DATE.—The amendments made by this section shall apply to electricity produced and sold after the date of the enactment of this Act, in taxable years ending after such date.

SEC. 103. ENERGY CREDIT.

(a) EXTENSION OF CREDIT.—

(1) SOLAR ENERGY PROPERTY.—Paragraphs (2)(A)(i)(II) and (3)(A)(ii) of section 48(a) are each amended by striking "January 1, 2009" and inserting "January 1, 2017".

(2) FUEL CELL PROPERTY.—Subparagraph (E) of section 48(c)(1) is amended by striking "December 31, 2008" and inserting "December 31, 2016".

(3) MICROTURBINE PROPERTY.—Subparagraph (E) of section 48(c)(2) is amended by striking "December 31, 2008" and inserting "December 31, 2016".

(b) ALLOWANCE OF ENERGY CREDIT AGAINST ALTERNATIVE MINIMUM TAX.—

(1) IN GENERAL.—Subparagraph (B) of section 38(c)(4), as amended by the Housing Assistance Tax Act of 2008, is amended

by redesignating clause (vi) as clause (vi) and (vii), respectively, and by in serting after clause (iv) the following new clause:

"(v) the credit determined under section 46 to the extent that such credit is attributable to the energy credit determined under section 48,".

(2) TECHNICAL AMENDMENT.—Clause (vi) of section 38(c)(4)(B), as redesignated by paragraph (1), is amended by striking "section 47 to the extent attributable to" and inserting "section 46 to the extent that such credit is attributable to the rehabilitation credit under section 47, but only with respect to".

(c) ENERGY CREDIT FOR COMBINED HEAT AND POWER SYSTEM PROPERTY.—

(1) IN GENERAL.—Section 48(a)(3)(A) is amended by striking "or" at the end of clause (iii), by inserting "or" at the end of clause (iv), and by adding at the end the following new clause:

"(v) combined heat and power system property,".

(2) COMBINED HEAT AND POWER SYSTEM PROPERTY.—Subsection (c) of section 48 is amended—

(A) by striking "QUALIFIED FUEL CELL PROPERTY; QUALIFIED MICROTURBINE PROPERTY" in the heading and inserting "DEFINITIONS", and

(B) by adding at the end the following new paragraph:

"(3) COMBINED HEAT AND POWER SYSTEM PROPERTY.—

"(A) COMBINED HEAT AND POWER SYSTEM PROPERTY.—The term 'combined heat and power system property' means property comprising a system—

"(i) which uses the same energy source for the simultaneous or sequential generation of electrical power, mechanical shaft power, or both, in combination with the generation of steam or other forms of useful thermal energy (including heating and cooling applications),

"(ii) which produces—

"(I) at least 20 percent of its total useful energy in the form of thermal energy which is not used to produce electrical or mechanical power (or combination thereof), and

"(II) at least 20 percent of its total useful energy in the form of electrical or mechanical power (or combination thereof),

"(iii) the energy efficiency percentage of which exceeds 60 percent, and

"(iv) which is placed in service before January 1, 2017.

(B) LIMITATION.—

"(i) IN GENERAL.—In the case of combined heat and power system property with an electrical capacity in excess of the applicable capacity placed in service during the taxable year, the credit under subsection (a)(1) (determined without regard to this paragraph) for such year shall be equal to the amount which bears the same ratio to such credit as the applicable capacity bears to the capacity of such property.

"(ii) APPLICABLE CAPACITY.—For purposes of clause (i), the term 'applicable capacity' means 15 megawatts or a mechanical energy capacity of more than 20,000 horse-power or an equivalent combination of electrical and mechanical energy capacities.

"(iii) MAXIMUM CAPACITY.—The term 'combined heat and power system property' shall not include any property comprising a system if such system has a capacity in excess of 50 megawatts or a mechanical energy capacity in excess of 67,000 horse-power or an equivalent combination of electrical and mechanical energy capacities.

"(C) SPECIAL RULES.—

"(i) ENERGY EFFICIENCY PERCENTAGE.—For purposes of this paragraph, the energy efficiency percentage of a system is the fraction—

"(I) the numerator of which is the total useful electrical, thermal, and mechanical power produced by the system at normal operating rates, and expected to be consumed in its normal application, and

"(II) the denominator of which is the lower heating value of the fuel sources for the system.

"(ii) DETERMINATIONS MADE ON BTU BASIS.—The energy efficiency percentage and the percentages under subparagraph (A)(ii) shall be determined on a Btu basis.

"(iii) INPUT AND OUTPUT PROPERTY NOT INCLUDED.—The term 'combined heat and power system property' does not include property used to transport the energy source to the facility or to distribute energy produced by the facility.

"(D) SYSTEMS USING BIOMASS.—If a system is designed to use biomass (within the meaning of paragraphs (2) and (3) of section 45(c) without regard to the last sentence of paragraph (3)(A)) for at least 90 percent of the energy source—

"(i) subparagraph (A)(iii) shall not apply, but

"(ii) the amount of credit determined under subsection (a) with respect to such system shall not exceed the amount which bears the same ratio to such amount of credit (determined without regard to this subparagraph) as the energy efficiency percentage of such system bears to 60 percent.".

(3) CONFORMING AMENDMENT.—Section 48(a)(1) is amended by striking "paragraphs (1)(B) and (2)(B)" and inserting "paragraphs (1)(B), (2)(B), and (3)(B)".

(d) INCREASE OF CREDIT LIMITATION FOR FUEL CELL PROPERTY.—Subparagraph (B) of section 48(c)(1) is amended by striking "$500" and inserting "$1,500".

(e) PUBLIC UTILITY PROPERTY TAKEN INTO ACCOUNT.—

(1) IN GENERAL.—Paragraph (3) of section 48(a) is amended by striking the second sentence thereof.

(2) CONFORMING AMENDMENTS.—

(A) Paragraph (1) of section 48(c) is amended by striking subparagraph (D) and re-designating subparagraph (E) as subparagraph (D).

(B) Paragraph (2) of section 48(c) is amended by striking subparagraph (D) and re-designating subparagraph (E) as subparagraph (D).

(f) EFFECTIVE DATE.—

(1) IN GENERAL.—Except as otherwise provided in this subsection, the amendments made by this section shall take effect on the date of the enactment of this Act.

(2) ALLOWANCE AGAINST ALTERNATIVE MINIMUM TAX.—The amendments made by subsection (b) shall apply to credits determined under section 46 of the Internal Revenue Code of 1986 in taxable years beginning after the date of the enactment of this Act and to carrybacks of such credits.

(3) COMBINED HEAT AND POWER AND FUEL CELL PROPERTY.—The amendments made by subsections (c) and (d) shall apply to periods after the date of the enactment of this Act, in taxable years ending after such date, under rules similar to the rules of section 48(m) of the Internal Revenue Code of 1986 (as in effect on the day before the date of the enactment of the Revenue Reconciliation Act of 1990).

(4) PUBLIC UTILITY PROPERTY.—The amendments made by subsection (e) shall apply to periods after February 13, 2008, in taxable years ending after such date, under rules similar to the rules of section 48(m) of the Internal Revenue Code of 1986 (as in effect on the day before the date of the enactment of the Revenue Reconciliation Act of 1990).

SEC. 104. ENERGY CREDIT FOR SMALL WIND PROPERTY.

(a) IN GENERAL.—Section 48(a)(3)(A), as amended by section 103, is amended by striking "or" at the end of clause (iv), by adding "or" at the end of clause (v), and by inserting after clause (v) the following new clause:

"(vi) qualified small wind energy property,".

(b) 30 PERCENT CREDIT.—Section 48(a)(2)(A)(i) is amended by striking "and" at the end of subclause (II) and by inserting after subclause (III) the following new subclause:

"(IV) qualified small wind energy property, and".

(c) QUALIFIED SMALL WIND ENERGY PROPERTY.— Section 48(c), as amended by section 103, is amended by adding at the end the following new paragraph:

"(4) QUALIFIED SMALL WIND ENERGY PROPERTY.—

"(A) IN GENERAL.—The term 'qualified small wind energy property' means property which uses a qualifying small wind turbine to generate electricity.

"(B) LIMITATION.—In the case of qualified small wind energy property placed in service during the taxable year, the credit otherwise determined under subsection (a)(1) for such year with respect to all such property of the taxpayer shall not exceed $4,000.

"(C) QUALIFYING SMALL WIND TURBINE.—The term 'qualifying small wind turbine' means a wind turbine which has a nameplate capacity of not more than 100 kilowatts.

"(D) TERMINATION.—The term 'qualified small wind energy property' shall not include any property for any period after December 31, 2016."

(d) CONFORMING AMENDMENT.—Section 48(a)(1), as amended by section 103, is amended by striking "paragraphs (1)(B), (2)(B), and (3)(B)" and inserting "paragraphs (1)(B), (2)(B), (3)(B), and (4)(B)".

(e) EFFECTIVE DATE.—The amendments made by this section shall apply to periods after the date of the enactment of this Act, in taxable years ending after such date, under rules similar to the rules of section 48(m) of the Internal Revenue Code of 1986 (as in effect on the day before the date of the enactment of the Revenue Reconciliation Act of 1990).

SEC. 105. ENERGY CREDIT FOR GEOTHERMAL HEAT PUMP SYSTEMS.

(a) IN GENERAL.—Subparagraph (A) of section 48(a)(3), as amended by this Act, is amended by striking "or" at the end of clause (v), by inserting "or" at the end of clause (vi), and by adding at the end the following new clause:

"(vii) equipment which uses the ground or ground water as a thermal energy source to heat a structure or as a thermal energy sink to cool a structure, but only with respect to periods ending before January 1, 2017,".

(b) EFFECTIVE DATE.—The amendments made by this section shall apply to periods after the date of the enactment of this Act, in taxable years ending after such date, under rules similar to the rules of section

48(m) of the Internal Revenue Code of 1986 (as in effect on the day before the date of the enactment of the Revenue Reconciliation Act of 1990).

SEC. 106. CREDIT FOR RESIDENTIAL ENERGY EFFICIENT PROPERTY.

(a) EXTENSION.—Section 25D(g) is amended by striking "December 31, 2008" and inserting "December 31, 2016".

(b) REMOVAL OF LIMITATION FOR SOLAR ELECTRIC PROPERTY.—

(1) IN GENERAL.—Section 25D(b)(1), as amended by subsections (c) and (d), is amended—

(A) by striking subparagraph (A), and

(B) by redesignating subparagraphs (B) through (E) as subparagraphs (A) through and (D), respectively.

(2) CONFORMING AMENDMENT.—Section 25D(e)(4)(A), as amended by subsections (c) and (d), is amended—

(A) by striking clause (i), and

(B) by redesignating clauses (ii) through (v) as clauses (i) and (iv), respectively.

(c) CREDIT FOR RESIDENTIAL WIND PROPERTY.—

(1) IN GENERAL.—Section 25D(a) is amended by striking "and" at the end of paragraph (2), by striking the period at the end of paragraph (3) and inserting ", and", and by adding at the end the following new paragraph:

"(4) 30 percent of the qualified small wind energy property expenditures made by the taxpayer during such year.".

(2) LIMITATION.—Section 25D(b)(1) is amended by striking "and" at the end of subparagraph (B), by striking the period at the end of subparagraph (C) and inserting ", and", and by adding at the end the following new subparagraph:

"(D) $500 with respect to each half kilowatt of capacity (not to exceed $4,000) of wind turbines for which qualified small wind energy property expenditures are made.".

(3) QUALIFIED SMALL WIND ENERGY PROPERTY EXPENDITURES.—

(A) IN GENERAL.—Section 25D(d) is amended by adding at the end the following new paragraph:

"(4) QUALIFIED SMALL WIND ENERGY PROPERTY EXPENDITURE.—The term 'qualified small wind energy property expenditure' means an expenditure for property which uses a wind turbine to generate electricity for use in connection with a dwelling unit located in the United States and used as a residence by the taxpayer.".

(B) NO DOUBLE BENEFIT.—Section 45(d)(1) is amended by adding at the end the following new sentence: "Such term shall not include any facility with respect to which any qualified small wind energy property expenditure (as defined in subsection (d)(4) of section 25D) is taken into account in determining the credit under such section.".

(4) MAXIMUM EXPENDITURES IN CASE OF JOINT OCCUPANCY.—Section 25D(e)(4)(A) is amended by striking "and" at the end of clause (ii), by striking the period at the end of clause (iii) and inserting ", and", and by adding at the end the following new clause:

"(iv) $1,667 in the case of each half kilowatt of capacity (not to exceed $13,333) of wind turbines for which qualified small wind energy property expenditures are made.".

(d) CREDIT FOR GEOTHERMAL HEAT PUMP SYSTEMS.—

(1) IN GENERAL.—Section 25D(a), as amended by subsection (c), is amended by striking "and" at the end of paragraph (3), by striking the period at the end of paragraph (4) and inserting ", and", and by adding at the end the following new paragraph:

"(5) 30 percent of the qualified geothermal heat pump property expenditures made by the taxpayer during such year.".

(2) LIMITATION.—Section 25D(b)(1), as amended by subsection (c), is amended by striking "and" at the end of subparagraph (C), by striking the period at the end of subparagraph (D) and inserting ", and", and by adding at the end the following new subparagraph:

"(E) $2,000 with respect to any qualified geothermal heat pump property expenditures.".

(3) QUALIFIED GEOTHERMAL HEAT PUMP PROPERTY EXPENDITURE.—Section 25D(d), as amended by subsection (c), is amended by adding at the end the following new paragraph:

"(5) QUALIFIED GEOTHERMAL HEAT PUMP PROPERTY EXPENDITURE.—

"(A) IN GENERAL.—The term 'qualified geothermal heat pump property expenditure' means an expenditure for qualified geothermal heat pump property installed on or in connection with a dwelling unit located in the United States and used as a residence by the taxpayer.

"(B) QUALIFIED GEOTHERMAL HEAT PUMP PROPERTY.—The term 'qualified geothermal heat pump property' means any equipment which—

"(i) uses the ground or ground water as a thermal energy source to heat the dwelling unit referred to in subparagraph (A) or as a thermal energy sink to cool such dwelling unit, and

"(ii) meets the requirements of the Energy Star program which are in effect at the time that the expenditure for such equipment is made.".

(4) MAXIMUM EXPENDITURES IN CASE OF JOINT OCCUPANCY.—Section 25D(e)(4)(A), as amended by subsection (c), is amended by striking

"and" at the end of clause (iii), by striking the period at the end of clause (iv) and inserting ", and", and by adding at the end the following new clause:

"(v) $6,667 in the case of any qualified geothermal heat pump property expenditures.".

(e) CREDIT ALLOWED AGAINST ALTERNATIVE MINIMUM TAX.—

(1) IN GENERAL.—Subsection (c) of section 25D is amended to read as follows:

"(c) LIMITATION BASED ON AMOUNT OF TAX; CARRYFORWARD OF UNUSED CREDIT.—

"(1) LIMITATION BASED ON AMOUNT OF TAX.—In the case of a taxable year to which section 26(a)(2) does not apply, the credit allowed under subsection (a) for the taxable year shall not exceed the excess of—

"(A) the sum of the regular tax liability (as defined in section 26(b)) plus the tax imposed by section 55, over

"(B) the sum of the credits allowable under this subpart (other than this section) and section 27 for the taxable year.

(2) CARRYFORWARD OF UNUSED CREDIT.—

"(A) RULE FOR YEARS IN WHICH ALL PERSONAL CREDITS ALLOWED AGAINST REGULAR AND ALTERNATIVE MINIMUM TAX.—In the case of a taxable year to which section 26(a)(2) applies, if the credit allowable under subsection (a) exceeds the limitation imposed by section 26(a)(2) for such taxable year reduced by the sum of the credits allowable under this subpart (other than this section), such excess shall be carried to the succeeding taxable year and added to the credit allowable under subsection (a) for such succeeding taxable year.

"(B) RULE FOR OTHER YEARS.—In the case of a taxable year to which section 26(a)(2) does not apply, if the credit allowable under subsection (a) exceeds the limitation imposed by paragraph (1) for such taxable year, such excess shall be carried to the succeeding taxable year and added to the credit allowable under subsection (a) for such succeeding taxable year.".

(2) CONFORMING AMENDMENTS.—

(A) Section 23(b)(4)(B) is amended by inserting "and section 25D" after "this section".

(B) Section 24(b)(3)(B) is amended by striking "and 25B" and inserting ", 25B, and 25D".

(C) Section 25B(g)(2) is amended by striking "section 23" and inserting "sections 23 and 25D".

(D) Section 26(a)(1) is amended by striking "and 25B" and inserting "25B, and 25D".

(f) EFFECTIVE DATE.—

156

(1) IN GENERAL.—Except as provided in paragraph (2), the amendments made by this section shall apply to taxable years beginning after December 31, 2007.

(2) SOLAR ELECTRIC PROPERTY LIMITATION.—The amendments made by subsection (b) shall apply to taxable years beginning after December 31, 2008.

(3) APPLICATION OF EGTRRA SUNSET.—The amendments made by subparagraphs (A) and (B) of subsection (e)(2) shall be subject to title IX of the Economic Growth and Tax Relief Reconciliation Act of 2001 in the same manner as the provisions of such Act to which such amendments relate.

SEC. 107. NEW CLEAN RENEWABLE ENERGY BONDS.

(a) IN GENERAL.—Subpart I of part IV of subchapter A of chapter 1 is amended by adding at the end the following new section:

"SEC. 54C. NEW CLEAN RENEWABLE ENERGY BONDS.

"(a) NEW CLEAN RENEWABLE ENERGY BOND.—For purposes of this subpart, the term 'new clean renewable energy bond' means any bond issued as part of an issue if—

"(1) 100 percent of the available project proceeds of such issue are to be used for capital expenditures incurred by governmental bodies, public power providers, or cooperative electric companies for one or more qualified renewable energy facilities,

"(2) the bond is issued by a qualified issuer, and

"(3) the issuer designates such bond for purposes of this section.

"(b) REDUCED CREDIT AMOUNT.—The annual credit determined under section 54A(b) with respect to any new clean renewable energy bond shall be 70 percent of the amount so determined without regard to this subsection.

"(c) LIMITATION ON AMOUNT OF BONDS DESIGNATED.—

"(1) IN GENERAL.—The maximum aggregate face amount of bonds which may be designated under subsection (a) by any issuer shall not exceed the limitation amount allocated under this subsection to such issuer.

"(2) NATIONAL LIMITATION ON AMOUNT OF BONDS DESIGNATED.—There is a national new clean renewable energy bond limitation of $800,000,000 which shall be allocated by the Secretary as provided in paragraph (3), except that—

"(A) not more than $33\frac{1}{3}$ percent thereof may be allocated to qualified projects of public power providers,

"(B) not more than 33⅓ percent thereof may be allocated to qualified projects of governmental bodies, and

"(C) not more than 33⅓ percent thereof may be allocated to qualified projects of cooperative electric companies.

"(3) METHOD OF ALLOCATION.—

"(A) ALLOCATION AMONG PUBLIC POWER PROVIDERS.—After the Secretary determines the qualified projects of public power providers which are appropriate for receiving an allocation of the national new clean renewable energy bond limitation, the Secretary shall, to the maximum extent practicable, make allocations among such projects in such manner that the amount allocated to each such project bears the same ratio to the cost of such project as the limitation under paragraph (2)(A) bears to the cost of all such projects.

"(B) ALLOCATION AMONG GOVERNMENTAL BODIES AND COOPERATIVE ELECTRIC COMPANIES.—The Secretary shall make allocations of the amount of the national new clean renewable energy bond limitation described in paragraphs (2)(B) and (2)(C) among qualified projects of governmental bodies and cooperative electric companies, respectively, in such manner as the Secretary determines appropriate.

"(d) DEFINITIONS.—For purposes of this section—

"(1) QUALIFIED RENEWABLE ENERGY FACILITY.—The term 'qualified renewable energy facility' means a qualified facility (as determined under section 45(d) without regard to paragraphs (8) and (10) thereof and to any placed in service date) owned by a public power provider, a governmental body, or a cooperative electric company.

"(2) PUBLIC POWER PROVIDER.—The term 'public power provider' means a State utility with a service obligation, as such terms are defined in section 217 of the Federal Power Act (as in effect on the date of the enactment of this paragraph).

"(3) GOVERNMENTAL BODY.—The term 'governmental body' means any State or Indian tribal government, or any political subdivision thereof.

"(4) COOPERATIVE ELECTRIC COMPANY.—The term 'cooperative electric company' means a mutual or cooperative electric company described in section 501(c)(12) or section 1381(a)(2)(C).

"(5) CLEAN RENEWABLE ENERGY BOND LENDER.—The term 'clean renewable energy bond lender' means a lender which is a cooperative which is owned by, or has outstanding loans to, 100 or more cooperative electric companies and is in existence on February 1, 2002, and shall include any affiliated entity which is controlled by such lender.

"(6) QUALIFIED ISSUER.—The term 'qualified issuer' means a public power provider, a cooperative electric company, a governmental body, a clean renewable energy bond lender, or a not-for-profit electric utility which has received a loan or loan guarantee under the Rural Electrification Act.".

(b) CONFORMING AMENDMENTS.—

(1) Paragraph (1) of section 54A(d) is amended to read as follows:

"(1) QUALIFIED TAX CREDIT BOND.—The term 'qualified tax credit bond' means—

"(A) a qualified forestry conservation bond, or

"(B) a new clean renewable energy bond, which is part of an issue that meets requirements of paragraphs (2), (3), (4), (5), and (6).".

(2) Subparagraph (C) of section 54A(d)(2) is amended to read as follows:

"(C) QUALIFIED PURPOSE.—For purposes of this paragraph, the term 'qualified purpose' means—

"(i) in the case of a qualified forestry conservation bond, a purpose specified in section 54B(e), and

"(ii) in the case of a new clean renewable energy bond, a purpose specified in section 54C(a)(1).".

(3) The table of sections for subpart I of part IV of subchapter A of chapter 1 is amended by adding at the end the following new item:

"SEC. 54C. QUALIFIED CLEAN RENEWABLE ENERGY BONDS.".

(c) EXTENSION FOR CLEAN RENEWABLE ENERGY BONDS.—Subsection (m) of section 54 is amended by striking "December 31, 2008" and inserting "December 31, 2009".

(d) EFFECTIVE DATE.—The amendments made by this section shall apply to obligations issued after the date of the enactment of this Act.

SEC. 108. CREDIT FOR STEEL INDUSTRY FUEL.

(a) TREATMENT AS REFINED COAL.—

(1) IN GENERAL.—Subparagraph (A) of section 45(c)(7) of the Internal Revenue Code of 1986 (relating to refined coal), as amended by this Act, is amended to read as follows:

"(A) IN GENERAL.—The term 'refined coal' means a fuel—

"(i) which—

"(I) is a liquid, gaseous, or solid fuel produced from coal (including lignite) or high carbon fly ash, including such fuel used as a feedstock,

"(II) is sold by the taxpayer with the reasonable expectation that it will be used for purpose of producing steam,

"(III) is certified by the taxpayer as resulting (when used in the production of steam) in a qualified emission reduction, and

"(IV) is produced in such a manner as to result in an increase of at least 50 percent in the market value of the refined coal (excluding any increase caused by materials combined or added during the production process), as compared to the value of the feedstock coal, or

"(ii) which is steel industry fuel.".

(2) STEEL INDUSTRY FUEL DEFINED.—Paragraph (7) of section 45(c) of such Code is amended by adding at the end the following new subparagraph:

(C) STEEL INDUSTRY FUEL.—

"(i) IN GENERAL.—The term 'steel industry fuel' means a fuel which—

"(I) is produced through a process of liquifying coal waste sludge and distributing it on coal, and

"(II) is used as a feedstock for the manufacture of coke.

"(ii) COAL WASTE SLUDGE.—The term 'coal waste sludge' means the tar decanter sludge and related byproducts of the coking process, including such materials that have been stored in ground, in tanks and in lagoons, that have been treated as hazardous wastes under applicable Federal environmental rules absent liquefaction and processing with coal into a feedstock for the manufacture of coke.".

(b) CREDIT AMOUNT.—

(1) IN GENERAL.—Paragraph (8) of section 45(e) of the Internal Revenue Code of 1986 (relating to refined coal production facilities) is amended by adding at the end the following new subparagraph

(D) SPECIAL RULE FOR STEEL INDUSTRY FUEL.—

"(i) IN GENERAL.—In the case of a taxpayer who produces steel industry fuel—

"(I) this paragraph shall be applied separately with respect to steel industry fuel and other refined coal, and

"(II) in applying this paragraph to steel industry fuel, the modifications in clause (ii) shall apply.

"(ii) MODIFICATIONS.—

"(I) CREDIT AMOUNT.—Subparagraph (A) shall be applied by substituting '$2 per barrel-of-oil equivalent' for '$4.375 per ton'.

"(II) CREDIT PERIOD.—In lieu of the 10-year period referred to in clauses (i) and (ii)(II) of subparagraph

160

(A), the credit period shall be the period beginning on the later of the date such facility was originally placed in service, the date the modifications described in clause (iii) were placed in service, or October 1, 2008, and ending on the later of December 31, 2009, or the date which is 1 year after the date such facility or the modifications described in clause (iii) were placed in service.

"(III) No PHASEOUT.—Subparagraph (B) shall not apply.

"(iii) MODIFICATIONS.—The modifications described in this clause are modifications to an existing facility which allow such facility to produce steel industry fuel.

"(iv) BARREL-OF-OIL EQUIVALENT.—For purposes of this subparagraph, a barrel-of-oil equivalent is the amount of steel industry fuel that has a Btu content of 5,800,000 Btus.".

(2) INFLATION ADJUSTMENT.—Paragraph (2) of section 45(b) of such Code is amended by inserting "the $3 amount in subsection (e)(8)(D)(ii)(I)," after "subsection (e)(8)(A),".

(c) TERMINATION.—Paragraph (8) of section 45(d) of the Internal Revenue Code of 1986 (relating to refined coal production facility), as amended by this Act, is amended to read as follows:

"(8) REFINED COAL PRODUCTION FACILITY.— In the case of a facility that produces refined coal, the term 'refined coal production facility' means—

"(A) with respect to a facility producing steel industry fuel, any facility (or any modification to a facility) which is placed in service before January 1, 2010, and

"(B) with respect to any other facility producing refined coal, any facility placed in service after the date of the enactment of the American Jobs Creation Act of 2004 and before January 1, 2010.".

(d) COORDINATION WITH CREDIT FOR PRODUCING FUEL FROM A NONCONVENTIONAL SOURCE.—

(1) IN GENERAL.—Subparagraph (B) of section 45(e)(9) of the Internal Revenue Code of 1986 is amended—

(A) by striking "The term" and inserting the following:
"(i) IN GENERAL.—The term", and

(B) by adding at the end the following new clause:
"(ii) EXCEPTION FOR STEEL INDUSTRY COAL.—In the case of a facility producing steel industry fuel, clause (i) shall not apply to so much of the refined coal produced at such facility as is steel industry fuel.".

161

(2) No DOUBLE BENEFIT.—Section 45K(g)(2) of such Code is amended by adding at the end the following new subparagraph:

"(E) COORDINATION WITH SECTION 45.— No credit shall be allowed with respect to any qualified fuel which is steel industry fuel (as defined in section 45(c)(7)) if a credit is allowed to the taxpayer for such fuel under section 45.".

(e) EFFECTIVE DATE.—The amendments made by this section shall apply to fuel produced and sold after September 30, 2008.

SEC. 109. SPECIAL RULE TO IMPLEMENT FERC AND STATE ELECTRIC RESTRUCTURING POLICY.

(a) EXTENSION FOR QUALIFIED ELECTRIC UTILITIES.—

(1) IN GENERAL.—Paragraph (3) of section 451(i) is amended by inserting "(before January 1, 2010, in the case of a qualified electric utility)" after "January 1, 2008".

(2) QUALIFIED ELECTRIC UTILITY.—Subsection (i) of section 451 is amended by redesignating paragraphs (6) through (10) as paragraphs (7) through (11), respectively, and by inserting after paragraph (5) the following new paragraph:

(6) QUALIFIED ELECTRIC UTILITY.—For purposes of this subsection, the term 'qualified electric utility' means a person that, as of the date of the qualifying electric transmission transaction, is vertically integrated, in that it is both—

(A) a transmitting utility (as defined in section 3(23) of the Federal Power Act (16 U.S.C. 796(23))) with respect to the transmission facilities to which the election under this subsection applies, and

"(B) an electric utility (as defined in section 3(22) of the Federal Power Act (16 U.S.C. 796(22))).".

(b) EXTENSION OF PERIOD FOR TRANSFER OF OPERATIONAL CONTROL AUTHORIZED BY FERC.— Clause (ii) of section 451(i)(4)(B) is amended by striking "December 31, 2007" and inserting "the date which is 4 years after the close of the taxable year in which the transaction occurs".

(c) PROPERTY LOCATED OUTSIDE THE UNITED STATES NOT TREATED AS EXEMPT UTILITY PROPERTY.—Paragraph (5) of section 451(i) is amended by adding at the end the following new subparagraph:

"(C) EXCEPTION FOR PROPERTY LOCATED OUTSIDE THE UNITED STATES.—The term 'exempt utility property' shall not include any property which is located outside the United States.".

(d) EFFECTIVE DATES.—

(1) EXTENSION.—The amendments made by subsection (a) shall apply to transactions after December 31, 2007.

(2) TRANSFERS OF OPERATIONAL CONTROL.— The amendment made by subsection (b) shall take effect as if included in section 909 of the American Jobs Creation Act of 2004.

(3) EXCEPTION FOR PROPERTY LOCATED OUTSIDE THE UNITED STATES.— The amendment made by subsection (c) shall apply to transactions after the date of the enactment of this Act.

Subtitle B—Carbon Mitigation and Coal Provisions

SEC. 111. EXPANSION AND MODIFICATION OF ADVANCED COAL PROJECT INVESTMENT CREDIT.

(a) MODIFICATION OF CREDIT AMOUNT.—Section 48A(a) is amended by striking "and" at the end of paragraph (1), by striking the period at the end of paragraph (2) and inserting ", and", and by adding at the end the following new paragraph:

"(3) 30 percent of the qualified investment for such taxable year in the case of projects described in clause (iii) of subsection (d)(3)(B).".

(b) EXPANSION OF AGGREGATE CREDITS.—Section 48A(d)(3)(A) is amended by striking "$1,300,000,000" and inserting "$2,550,000,000".

(c) AUTHORIZATION OF ADDITIONAL PROJECTS.—

(1) IN GENERAL.—Subparagraph (B) of section 48A(d)(3) is amended to read as follows:

"(B) PARTICULAR PROJECTS.—Of the dollar amount in subparagraph (A), the Secretary is authorized to certify—

"(i) $800,000,000 for integrated gasification combined cycle projects the application for which is submitted during the period described in paragraph (2)(A)(i),

"(ii) $500,000,000 for projects which use other advanced coal-based generation technologies the application for which is submitted during the period described in paragraph (2)(A)(i), and

"(iii) $1,250,000,000 for advanced coal-based generation technology projects the application for which is submitted during the period described in paragraph (2)(A)(ii)."

(2) APPLICATION PERIOD FOR ADDITIONAL PROJECTS.—Subparagraph (A) of section 48A(d)(2) is amended to read as follows:

"(A) APPLICATION PERIOD.—Each applicant for certification under this paragraph shall submit an application meeting the requirements of subparagraph (B). An applicant may only submit an application—

"(i) for an allocation from the dollar amount specified in clause (i) or (ii) of paragraph (3)(B) during the 3-year period beginning on the date the Secretary establishes the program under paragraph (1), and

"(ii) for an allocation from the dollar amount specified in paragraph (3)(B)(iii) during the 3-year period beginning at the earlier of the termination of the period described in clause (i) or the date prescribed by the Secretary."

(3) CAPTURE AND SEQUESTRATION OF CARBON DIOXIDE EMISSIONS REQUIREMENT.—

(A) IN GENERAL.—Section 48A(e)(1) is amended by striking "and" at the end of sub-paragraph (E), by striking the period at the end of subparagraph (F) and inserting "; and", and by adding at the end the following new sub-paragraph:

"(G) in the case of any project the application for which is submitted during the period described in subsection (d)(2)(A)(ii), the project includes equipment which separates and sequesters at least 65 percent (70 percent in the case of an application for reallocated credits under subsection (d)(4)) of such project's total carbon dioxide emissions.".

(B) HIGHEST PRIORITY FOR PROJECTS WHICH SEQUESTER CARBON DIOXIDE EMISSIONS.—Section 48A(e)(3) is amended by striking "and" at the end of subparagraph (A)(iii), by striking the period at the end of subparagraph (B)(iii) and inserting ", and", and by adding at the end the following new subparagraph:

"(C) give highest priority to projects with the greatest separation and sequestration percentage of total carbon dioxide emissions.".

(C) RECAPTURE OF CREDIT FOR FAILURE TO SEQUESTER.—Section 48A is amended by adding at the end the following new subsection:

"(i) RECAPTURE OF CREDIT FOR FAILURE TO SEQUESTER.—The Secretary shall provide for recapturing the benefit of any credit allowable under subsection (a) with respect to any project which fails to attain or maintain the separation and sequestration requirements of subsection (e)(1)(G)."

(4) ADDITIONAL PRIORITY FOR RESEARCH PARTNERSHIPS.—Section 48A(e)(3)(B), as amended by paragraph (3)(B), is amended—

(A) by striking "and" at the end of clause (ii),

(B) by redesignating clause (iii) as clause (iv), and

(C) by inserting after clause (ii) the following new clause:

"(iii) applicant participants who have a research partnership with an eligible educational institution (as defined in section 529(e)(5)), and".

(5) CLERICAL AMENDMENT.—Section 48A(e)(3) is amended by striking "INTEGRATED GASIFICATION COMBINED CYCLE" in the heading and inserting "CERTAIN".

(d) DISCLOSURE OF ALLOCATIONS.—Section 48A(d) is amended by adding at the end the following new paragraph:

"(5) DISCLOSURE OF ALLOCATIONS.—The Secretary shall, upon making a certification under this subsection or section 48B(d), publicly disclose the identity of the applicant and the amount of the credit certified with respect to such applicant.".

(e) EFFECTIVE DATES.—

(1) IN GENERAL.—Except as otherwise provided in this subsection, the amendments made by this section shall apply to credits the application for which is submitted during the period described in section 48A(d)(2)(A)(ii) of the Internal Revenue Code of 1986 and which are allocated or reallocated after the date of the enactment of this Act.

(2) DISCLOSURE OF ALLOCATIONS.—The amendment made by subsection (d) shall apply to certifications made after the date of the enactment of this Act.

(3) CLERICAL AMENDMENT.—The amendment made by subsection (c)(5) shall take effect as if included in the amendment made by section 1307(b) of the Energy Tax Incentives Act of 2005.

SEC. 112. EXPANSION AND MODIFICATION OF COAL GASIFICATION INVESTMENT CREDIT.

(a) MODIFICATION OF CREDIT AMOUNT.—Section 48B(a) is amended by inserting "(30 percent in the case of credits allocated under subsection (d)(1)(B))" after "20 percent".

(b) EXPANSION OF AGGREGATE CREDITS.—Section 48B(d)(1) is amended by striking "shall not exceed $350,000,000" and all that follows and inserting "shall not exceed—

"(A) $350,000,000, plus

"(B) $250,000,000 for qualifying gasification projects that include equipment which separates and sequesters at least 75 percent of such project's total carbon dioxide emissions.".

(c) RECAPTURE OF CREDIT FOR FAILURE TO SEQUESTER.—Section 48B is amended by adding at the end the following new subsection:

"(f) RECAPTURE OF CREDIT FOR FAILURE TO SEQUESTER.—The Secretary shall provide for recapturing the benefit of any credit allowable under subsection (a) with respect to any project which fails to attain or maintain the separation and sequestration requirements for such project under subsection (d)(1).".

(d) SELECTION PRIORITIES.—Section 48B(d) is amended by adding at the end the following new paragraph:

"(4) SELECTION PRIORITIES.—In determining which qualifying gasification projects to certify under this section, the Secretary shall—

"(A) give highest priority to projects with the greatest separation and sequestration percentage of total carbon dioxide emissions, and

"(B) give high priority to applicant participants who have a research partnership with an eligible educational institution (as defined in section 529(e)(5)).".

(e) ELIGIBLE PROJECTS INCLUDE TRANSPORTATION GRADE LIQUID FUELS.—Section 48B(c)(7) (defining eligible entity) is amended by striking "and" at the end of subparagraph (F), by striking the period at the end of subparagraph (G) and inserting ", and", and by adding at the end the following new subparagraph:

"(H) transportation grade liquid fuels.".

(f) EFFECTIVE DATE.—The amendments made by this section shall apply to credits described in section 48B(d)(1)(B) of the Internal Revenue Code of 1986 which are allocated or reallocated after the date of the enactment of this Act.

SEC. 113. TEMPORARY INCREASE IN COAL EXCISE TAX; FUNDING OF BLACK LUNG DISABILITY TRUST FUND.

(a) EXTENSION OF TEMPORARY INCREASE.—Paragraph (2) of section 4121(e) is amended—

(1) by striking "January 1, 2014" in subparagraph (A) and inserting "December 31, 2018", and by (2) striking "January 1 after 1981" in subparagraph (B) and inserting "December 31 after 2007".

(b) RESTRUCTURING OF TRUST FUND DEBT.—

(1) DEFINITIONS.—For purposes of this subsection—

(A) MARKET VALUE OF THE OUTSTANDING REPAYABLE ADVANCES, PLUS ACCRUED INTEREST.—The term "market value of the outstanding repayable advances, plus accrued interest" means the present value (determined by the Secretary of the Treasury as of the refinancing date and using the Treasury rate as the discount rate) of the stream of principal and interest payments derived assuming that each repayable advance that is outstanding on the refinancing date is due on the 30th anniversary of the end of the fiscal year in which the advance was made to the Trust Fund, and that all such principal and interest payments are made on September 30 of the applicable fiscal year.

(B) REFINANCING DATE.—The term "refinancing date" means the date occurring 2 days after the enactment of this Act.

(C) REPAYABLE ADVANCE.—The term "repayable advance" means an amount that has been appropriated to the Trust Fund in order to make benefit payments and other expenditures that are authorized under section 9501 of the Internal Revenue Code of 1986 and are required to be repaid when the Secretary of the Treasury determines that monies are available in the Trust Fund for such purpose.

(D) TREASURY RATE.—The term "Treasury rate" means a rate determined by the Secretary of the Treasury, taking into consideration current market yields on outstanding marketable obligations of the United States of comparable maturities.

(E) TREASURY 1-YEAR RATE.—The term "Treasury 1-year rate" means a rate determined by the Secretary of the Treasury, taking into consideration current market yields on outstanding marketable obligations of the United States with remaining periods to maturity of approximately 1 year, to have been in effect as of the close of business 1 business day prior to the date on which the Trust Fund issues obligations to the Secretary of the Treasury under paragraph (2)(B).

(F) TRUST FUND.—The term "Trust Fund" means the Black Lung Disability Trust Fund established under section 9501 of the Internal Revenue Code of 1986.

(2) REFINANCING OF OUTSTANDING PRINCIPAL OF REPAYABLE ADVANCES AND UNPAID INTEREST ON SUCH ADVANCES.—

(A) TRANSFER TO GENERAL FUND.—On the refinancing date, the Trust Fund shall repay the market value of the outstanding repayable advances, plus accrued interest, by transferring into the general fund of the Treasury the following sums:

(i) The proceeds from obligations that the Trust Fund shall issue to the Secretary of the Treasury in such amounts as the Secretaries of Labor and the Treasury shall determine and bearing interest at the Treasury rate, and that shall be in such forms and denominations and be subject to such other terms and conditions, including maturity, as the Secretary of the Treasury shall prescribe.

(ii) All, or that portion, of the appropriation made to the Trust Fund pursuant to paragraph (3) that is needed to cover the difference defined in that paragraph.

(B) REPAYMENT OF OBLIGATIONS.—In the event that the Trust Fund is unable to repay the obligations that it has issued to the Secretary of the Treasury under subparagraph (A)(i) and this subparagraph, or is unable to make benefit payments and other authorized expenditures, the Trust Fund shall issue obligations to the Secretary of the Treasury in such amounts as may be necessary to make such repayments,

payments, and expenditures, with a maturity of 1 year, and bearing interest at the Treasury 1-year rate. These obligations shall be in such forms and denominations and be subject to such other terms and conditions as the Secretary of the Treasury shall prescribe.

(C) AUTHORITY TO ISSUE OBLIGATIONS.—The Trust Fund is authorized to issue obligations to the Secretary of the Treasury under subparagraphs (A)(i) and (B). The Secretary of the Treasury is authorized to purchase such obligations of the Trust Fund. For the purposes of making such purchases, the Secretary of the Treasury may use as a public debt transaction the proceeds from the sale of any securities issued under chapter 31 of title 31, United States Code, and the purposes for which securities may be issued under such chapter are extended to include any purchase of such Trust Fund obligations under this subparagraph.

(3) ONE-TIME APPROPRIATION.—There is hereby appropriated to the Trust Fund an amount sufficient to pay to the general fund of the Treasury the difference between—

(A) the market value of the outstanding repayable advances, plus accrued interest; and

(B) the proceeds from the obligations issued by the Trust Fund to the Secretary of the Treasury under paragraph (2)(A)(i).

(4) PREPAYMENT OF TRUST FUND OBLIGATIONS.—The Trust Fund is authorized to repay any obligation issued to the Secretary of the Treasury under subparagraphs (A)(i) and (B) of paragraph (2) prior to its maturity date by paying a prepayment price that would, if the obligation being prepaid (including all unpaid interest accrued thereon through the date of prepayment) were purchased by a third party and held to the maturity date of such obligation, produce a yield to the third-party purchaser for the period from the date of purchase to the maturity date of such obligation substantially equal to the Treasury yield on outstanding marketable obligations of the United States having a comparable maturity to this period.

SEC. 114. SPECIAL RULES FOR REFUND OF THE COAL EXCISE TAX TO CERTAIN COAL PRODUCERS AND EXPORTERS.

(a) REFUND.—

(1) COAL PRODUCERS.—

(A) IN GENERAL.—Notwithstanding subsections (a)(1) and (c) of section 6416 and section 6511 of the Internal Revenue Code of 1986, if—

(i) a coal producer establishes that such coal producer, or a party related to such coal producer, exported coal produced by such coal producer to a foreign country or shipped coal produced by such coal producer to a possession of the United States, or caused such coal to be exported or shipped, the export or shipment of which was other than through an exporter who meets the requirements of paragraph (2),

(ii) such coal producer filed an excise tax return on or after October 1, 1990, and on or before the date of the enactment of this Act, and

(iii) such coal producer files a claim for refund with the Secretary not later than the close of the 30-day period beginning on the date of the enactment of this Act,

then the Secretary shall pay to such coal producer an amount equal to the tax paid under section 4121 of such Code on such coal exported or shipped by the coal producer or a party related to such coal producer, or caused by the coal producer or a party related to such coal producer to be exported or shipped.

(B) SPECIAL RULES FOR CERTAIN TAXPAYERS.—For purposes of this section—

(i) IN GENERAL.—If a coal producer or a party related to a coal producer has received a judgment described in clause (iii), such coal producer shall be deemed to have established the export of coal to a foreign country or shipment of coal to a possession of the United States under sub-paragraph (A)(i).

(ii) AMOUNT OF PAYMENT.—If a taxpayer described in clause (i) is entitled to a payment under subparagraph (A), the amount of such payment shall be reduced by any amount paid pursuant to the judgment described in clause (iii).

(iii) JUDGMENT DESCRIBED.—A judgment is described in this subparagraph if such judgment—

(I) is made by a court of competent jurisdiction within the United States,

(II) relates to the constitutionality of any tax paid on exported coal under section 4121 of the Internal Revenue Code of 1986, and

(III) is in favor of the coal producer or the party related to the coal producer.

(2) EXPORTERS.—Notwithstanding subsections (a)(1) and (c) of section 6416 and section 6511 of the Internal Revenue Code of 1986, and a judgment described in paragraph (1)(B)(iii) of this subsection, if—

(A) an exporter establishes that such exporter exported coal to a foreign country or shipped coal to a possession of the United States, or caused such coal to be so exported or shipped,

(B) such exporter filed a tax return on or after October 1, 1990, and on or before the date of the enactment of this Act, and

(C) such exporter files a claim for refund with the Secretary not later than the close of the 30-day period beginning on the date of the enactment of this Act,

then the Secretary shall pay to such exporter an amount equal to $0.825 per ton of such coal exported by the exporter or caused to be exported or shipped, or caused to be exported or shipped, by the exporter.

(b) LIMITATIONS.—Subsection (a) shall not apply with respect to exported coal if a settlement with the Federal Government has been made with and accepted by, the coal producer, a party related to such coal producer, or the exporter, of such coal, as of the date that the claim is filed under this section with respect to such exported coal. For purposes of this subsection, the term "settlement with the Federal Government" shall not include any settlement or stipulation entered into as of the date of the enactment of this Act, the terms of which contemplate a judgment concerning which any party has reserved the right to file an appeal, or has filed an appeal.

(c) SUBSEQUENT REFUND PROHIBITED.—No refund shall be made under this section to the extent that a credit or refund of such tax on such exported or shipped coal has been paid to any person.

(d) DEFINITIONS.—For purposes of this section—

(1) COAL PRODUCER.—The term "coal producer" means the person in whom is vested ownership of the coal immediately after the coal is severed from the ground, without regard to the existence of any contractual arrangement for the sale or other disposition of the coal or the payment of any royalties between the producer and third parties. The term includes any person who extracts coal from coal waste refuse piles or from the silt waste product which results from the wet washing (or similar processing) of coal.

(2) EXPORTER.—The term "exporter" means a person, other than a coal producer, who does not have a contract, fee arrangement, or any other agreement with a producer or seller of such coal to export or ship such coal to a third party on behalf of the producer or seller of such coal and—

(A) is indicated in the shipper's export declaration or other documentation as the exporter of record, or

(B) actually exported such coal to a foreign country or shipped such coal to a possession of the United States, or caused such coal to be so exported or shipped.

(3) RELATED PARTY.—The term "a party related to such coal producer" means a person who—

    (A) is related to such coal producer through any degree of common management, stock ownership, or voting control,

    (B) is related (within the meaning of section 144(a)(3) of the Internal Revenue Code of 1986) to such coal producer, or

    (C) has a contract, fee arrangement, or any other agreement with such coal producer to sell such coal to a third party on behalf of such coal producer.

(4) SECRETARY.—The term "Secretary" means the Secretary of Treasury or the Secretary's designee.

(e) TIMING OF REFUND.—With respect to any claim for refund filed pursuant to this section, the Secretary shall determine whether the requirements of this section are met not later than 180 days after such claim is filed. If the Secretary determines that the requirements of this section are met, the claim for refund shall be paid not later than 180 days after the Secretary makes such determination.

(f) INTEREST.—Any refund paid pursuant to this section shall be paid by the Secretary with interest from the date of overpayment determined by using the overpayment rate and method under section 6621 of the Internal Revenue Code of 1986.

(g) DENIAL OF DOUBLE BENEFIT.—The payment under subsection (a) with respect to any coal shall not exceed—

    (1) in the case of a payment to a coal producer, the amount of tax paid under section 4121 of the Internal Revenue Code of 1986 with respect to such coal by such coal producer or a party related to such coal producer, and

    (2) in the case of a payment to an exporter, an amount equal to $0.825 per ton with respect to such coal exported by the exporter or caused to be exported by the exporter.

(h) APPLICATION OF SECTION.—This section applies only to claims on coal exported or shipped on or after October 1, 1990, through the date of the enactment of this Act.

(i) STANDING NOT CONFERRED.—

    (1) EXPORTERS.—With respect to exporters, this section shall not confer standing upon an exporter to commence, or intervene in, any judicial or administrative proceeding concerning a claim for refund by a coal producer of any Federal or State tax, fee, or royalty paid by the coal producer.

    (2) COAL PRODUCERS.—With respect to coal producers, this section shall not confer standing upon a coal producer to commence, or intervene in, any judicial or administrative proceeding concerning a claim for refund by an exporter of any Federal or State tax, fee, or royalty paid by the producer and alleged to have been passed on to an exporter.

SEC. 115. TAX CREDIT FOR CARBON DIOXIDE SEQUESTRATION.

(a) IN GENERAL.—Subpart D of part IV of subchapter A of chapter 1 (relating to business credits) is amended by adding at the end the following new section:

"SEC. 45Q. CREDIT FOR CARBON DIOXIDE SEQUESTRATION.

"(a) GENERAL RULE.—For purposes of section 38, the carbon dioxide sequestration credit for any taxable year is an amount equal to the sum of—

"(1) $20 per metric ton of qualified carbon dioxide which is—

"(A) captured by the taxpayer at a qualified facility, and

"(B) disposed of by the taxpayer in secure geological storage, and

"(2) $10 per metric ton of qualified carbon dioxide which is—

"(A) captured by the taxpayer at a qualified facility, and

"(B) used by the taxpayer as a tertiary injectant in a qualified enhanced oil or natural gas recovery project.

"(b) QUALIFIED CARBON DIOXIDE.—For purposes of this section—

"(1) IN GENERAL.—The term 'qualified carbon dioxide' means carbon dioxide captured from an industrial source which—

"(A) would otherwise be released into the atmosphere as industrial emission of greenhouse gas, and

"(B) is measured at the source of capture and verified at the point of disposal or injection.

"(2) RECYCLED CARBON DIOXIDE.—The term 'qualified carbon dioxide' includes the initial deposit of captured carbon dioxide used as a tertiary injectant. Such term does not include carbon dioxide that is re-captured, recycled, and re-injected as part of the enhanced oil and natural gas recovery process.

"(c) QUALIFIED FACILITY.—For purposes of this section, the term 'qualified facility' means any industrial facility—

"(1) which is owned by the taxpayer,

"(2) at which carbon capture equipment is placed in service, and

"(3) which captures not less than 500,000 metric tons of carbon dioxide during the taxable year.

"(d) SPECIAL RULES AND OTHER DEFINITIONS.— For purposes of this section—

"(1) ONLY CARBON DIOXIDE CAPTURED AND DISPOSED OF OR USED WITHIN THE UNITED STATES TAKEN INTO ACCOUNT.—The credit under this section shall apply only with respect to qualified carbon dioxide the capture and disposal or use of which is within—

"(A) the United States (within the meaning of section 638(1)), or

172

"(B) a possession of the United States (within the meaning of section 638(2)).

"(2) SECURE GEOLOGICAL STORAGE.—The Secretary, in consultation with the Administrator of the Environmental Protection Agency, shall establish regulations for determining adequate security measures for the geological storage of carbon dioxide under subsection (a)(1)(B) such that the carbon dioxide does not escape into the atmosphere. Such term shall include storage at deep saline formations and unminable coal seams under such conditions as the Secretary may determine under such regulations.

"(3) TERTIARY INJECTANT.—The term 'tertiary injectant' has the same meaning as when used within section 193(b)(1).

"(4) QUALIFIED ENHANCED OIL OR NATURAL GAS RECOVERY PROJECT.—The term 'qualified enhanced oil or natural gas recovery project' has the meaning given the term 'qualified enhanced oil recovery project' by section 43(c)(2), by substituting 'crude oil or natural gas' for 'crude oil' in subparagraph (A)(i) thereof.

"(5) CREDIT ATTRIBUTABLE TO TAXPAYER.—Any credit under this section shall be attributable to the person that captures and physically or contractually ensures the disposal of or the use as a tertiary injectant of the qualified carbon dioxide, except to the extent provided in regulations prescribed by the Secretary.

"(6) RECAPTURE.—The Secretary shall, by regulations, provide for recapturing the benefit of any credit allowable under subsection (a) with respect to any qualified carbon dioxide which ceases to be captured, disposed of, or used as a tertiary injectant in a manner consistent with the requirements of this section.

"(7) INFLATION ADJUSTMENT.—In the case of any taxable year beginning in a calendar year after 2009, there shall be substituted for each dollar amount contained in subsection (a) an amount equal to the product of—

"(A) such dollar amount, multiplied by

"(B) the inflation adjustment factor for such calendar year determined under section 43(b)(3)(B) for such calendar year, determined by substituting '2008' for '1990'.

"(e) APPLICATION OF SECTION.—The credit under this section shall apply with respect to qualified carbon dioxide before the end of the calendar year in which the Secretary, in consultation with the Administrator of the Environmental Protection Agency, certifies that 75,000,000 metric tons of qualified carbon dioxide have been captured and disposed of or used as a tertiary injectant.".

(b) CONFORMING AMENDMENT.—Section 38(b) (relating to general business credit) is amended by striking "plus" at the end of paragraph

(32), by striking the period at the end of paragraph (33) and inserting ", plus", and by adding at the end of following new paragraph:

"(34) the carbon dioxide sequestration credit determined under section 45Q(a).".

(c) CLERICAL AMENDMENT.—The table of sections for subpart B of part IV of subchapter A of chapter 1 (relating to other credits) is amended by adding at the end the following new section:

"SEC. 45Q. CREDIT FOR CARBON DIOXIDE SEQUESTRATION.".

(d) EFFECTIVE DATE.—The amendments made by this section shall apply to carbon dioxide captured after the date of the enactment of this Act.

SEC. 116. CERTAIN INCOME AND GAINS RELATING TO INDUSTRIAL SOURCE CARBON DIOXIDE TREATED AS QUALIFYING INCOME FOR PUBLICLY TRADED PARTNERSHIPS.

(a) IN GENERAL.—Subparagraph (E) of section 7704(d)(1) (defining qualifying income) is amended by inserting "or industrial source carbon dioxide" after "timber)".

(b) EFFECTIVE DATE.—The amendment made by this section shall take effect on the date of the enactment of this Act, in taxable years ending after such date.

SEC. 117. CARBON AUDIT OF THE TAX CODE.

(a) STUDY.—The Secretary of the Treasury shall enter into an agreement with the National Academy of Sciences to undertake a comprehensive review of the Internal Revenue Code of 1986 to identify the types of and specific tax provisions that have the largest effects on carbon and other greenhouse gas emissions and to estimate the magnitude of those effects.

(b) REPORT.—Not later than 2 years after the date of enactment of this Act, the National Academy of Sciences shall submit to Congress a report containing the results of study authorized under this section.

(c) AUTHORIZATION OF APPROPRIATIONS.—There is authorized to be appropriated to carry out this section $1,500,000 for the period of fiscal years 2009 and 2010.

Amend the title so as to read: "To provide authority for the Federal Government to purchase and insure certain types of troubled assets for the purposes of providing stability to and preventing disruption in the economy and financial system and protecting taxpayers, to amend the Internal Revenue Code of 1986 to provide incentives for energy production and conservation, to extend certain expiring provisions, to provide individual income tax relief, and for other purposes".

Glossary of Terms and Agencies

If you are trying to understand the $700 billion bailout bill, the mortgage crisis, and Wall Street and you don't work in the financial services industry, the terms and agencies involved might sound like ancient Greek. But it's not all that complicated if you pay attention. The following are definitions of government agencies, different players in the mortgage industry, loan products, and other phrases that I hope will alleviate some of the confusion.

A credit quality or prime quality loan A mortgage where the borrower has the best credit rating possible, usually north of 700. Fannie Mae and Freddie Mac tend to buy these loans. (*See* credit score/FICO score.)

Alt-A mortgage (loan) A nonconforming mortgage where the borrower has a higher than subprime credit score. Alt-A is short for "alternative A." Typically, these loans may not be immediately eligible for purchase by Fannie Mae and Freddie Mac because they have underwriting anomalies that might include higher than normal debt-to-income ratios or irregular income. However, Fannie and Freddie have bought billions of dollars' worth of bonds backed by some alt-A loans.

asset-backed security (ABS) A bond backed by subprime loans. The term is used to distinguish these securities from bonds backed by Fannie Mae/Freddie-quality loans.

collateralized debt obligation (CDO) A bond created from tranches of other bonds. A tranche represents cash flow from a pool of different mortgages. In an attempt to diversify risk, a CDO might contain many different tranches from different asset-backed securities.

conventional or A credit quality mortgage (loan) A mortgage that meets underwriting standards dictated by Fannie Mae or Freddie Mac, two Congressionally chartered mortgage investing companies that provide liquidity to the market by purchasing loans from mortgage banking firms.

credit default swap (CDS) An instrument used to hedge against losses, or to speculate on the value of bonds (mortgages or otherwise). Credit default swaps act as an insurance policy of sorts where one party must pay another in the event the bonds lose value. The total credit default bets against a bond can actually outweigh the size of the bond being bet against. There are roughly $44 trillion in outstanding credit default swaps (bets) in the United States. It is an unregulated business, but that probably will change in the coming year.

credit score/FICO score A grade given to a consumer based on his or her credit history. A credit score involves a statistical analysis of a borrower's ability to pay. Credit scores were first developed by the Fair Isaac Corporation of Minneapolis. (In general, a subprime borrower is someone whose score is 620 or under. A paper borrowers have scores north of 700. If a borrower's credit is between those two numbers, he or she might be considered an alternative A (alt-A) or some other type of credit.

Department of Housing and Urban Development (HUD) A cabinet-level agency whose secretary is appointed by the president. HUD's job is to promote home ownership and administer the government's mortgage insurance program, the Federal Housing Administration (FHA). (*See* FHA/VA loan.)

Emergency Economic Stabilization Act (EESA) The bill signed into law by President Bush on October 3, 2008, that gives the U.S. Treasury the legal right to use $700 billion in taxpayer money to buy troubled mortgages (and other types of assets) from financial institutions. It also gives the Treasury the authority to buy ownership stakes in banks and Wall Street firms through the purchase of preferred stock. (Preferred stock carries a dividend, but the government under EESA will not have voting rights or hold board positions at banks.)

Fannie Mae Chartered by Congress, the Federal National Mortgage Association (FNMA) is a government-sponsored enterprise (GSE) whose mission is to provide liquidity (more money) to the mortgage market. Fannie does this by buying mortgages from lenders, giving them cash or a mortgage-backed bond they can sell for cash or even borrow against. Fannie Mae and its sibling company, Freddie Mac, found themselves in financial trouble in 2007 and 2008 when many of the subprime- and alt-A-backed bonds they invested in went delinquent in large numbers. Both are now wards of the government but still carry out the same mission of providing liquidity. Their long-term futures are uncertain.

Federal Deposit Insurance Corporation (FDIC) The regulator of most commercial banks. The FDIC also insures the deposits at the nation's banks and savings and loans. Under the EESA bill, the FDIC now insures deposits of up to $250,000 per account (an increase from the former maximum of $100,000). Recent temporary changes in federal rules make virtually all deposits federally insured.

Federal Housing Finance Agency (FHFA) The regulator of Fannie Mae and Freddie Mac. The FHFA is now managing both these mortgage investing giants under a federal conservatorship and has appointed new management teams to both. The federal takeover came on September 7, 2008. The common shares of Fannie and Freddie continue to trade on the New York Stock Exchange but are nearly worthless.

Federal Reserve The central bank of the United States. It is the Fed's job not only to set monetary policy (making decisions on increasing or cutting interest rates) but also to fight inflation. The Federal Reserve also lends money to banks in the form of short-term loans through what is called its discount window. Fed chairman Ben Bernanke worked closely with Treasury secretary

Henry Paulson in regard to how key aspects of EESA, especially the Troubled Asset Relief Program (TARP), would be carried out.

FHA Secure A loan program launched by the Federal Housing Administration (FHA) in early 2008 to help refinance troubled subprime borrowers into government-insured loans. The FHA is a government insurance program and part of the Department of Housing and Urban Development, a cabinet-level agency. For more information visit www.hud.gov/news/fhasecure.cfm.

FHA/VA loan A mortgage insured by one of two government agencies, either the Federal Housing Administration (FHA) or the Department of Veterans Affairs (VA). These loans often are packaged into bonds guaranteed by the Government National Mortgage Association (GNMA). The FHA and GNMA programs are administered by the Department of Housing and Urban Development, whose secretary is appointed by the president.

first lien (mortgage) The first deed of trust recorded against a house. Some consumers have two loans taken out against their house (or even three or four). The lien that is recorded first has priority over all other liens, which means that in the event of foreclosure if any money is recovered on the sale of the house the first lien holder gets paid before other debtors.

ForeclosureS.com A web site that offers free information—to some degree—on home foreclosures, including lists of foreclosures and information on state laws tied to the process. Searches can be done by zip code, county, or state. Some of its services are free, whereas others requirement payment. Web site address: www.foreclosures.com.

Freddie Mac The Federal Home Loan Mortgage Corporation (FHLMC) is a sibling company to Fannie Mae that also buys home mortgages from lenders. (*See also* Fannie Mae.)

Glass–Steagall Act Enacted during the Depression in 1933, this law prevented securities firms on Wall Street from owning banks and vice versa. Under Glass-Steagall, banks could not underwrite securities, including mortgage-backed bonds. Also, Wall Street firms could not offer federally insured deposits to the public, although they could serve as deposit brokers, funneling large chunks of certificates of deposit (CDs) into banks and savings and loans (S&Ls). In 1999 most of the prohibitions under Glass–Steagall ended with the passage of the Gramm–Leach–Bliley Act.

government–sponsored enterprise (GSE) An investment company chartered by the federal government to buy residential mortgages from banks, S&Ls, nondepository mortgage bankers, and others as a way to add liquidity to the market. Fannie Mae and Freddie Mac are the two largest GSEs serving the residential mortgage market. Even though they have government charters, the federal government does not, as a technical matter, insure their bonds, debt, or stock (though investors believe that in the event of defaults, the federal government would in fact guarantee payments).

hedge fund An unregulated for-profit company that manages money for individuals and institutional clients. Very few hedge funds are publicly traded, and they are not required to provide financial statements to the public or the Securities and Exchange Commission. These unregulated entities, however, buy and sell public securities, including stocks and bonds. Hedge funds also short stocks and speculate using such instruments as credit default swaps.

home equity loan A second deed of trust (or lien) that is taken out by a consumer on his or her home. There are two types of second liens: a closed-end loan for a fixed (set) amount or an open-end loan that has a cap but can be borrowed against in different increments.

Hope for Homeowners (H4H) program A government program run out of the Department of Housing and Urban Development. This program was created not by the Emergency Economic Stabilization Act but by a bill passed in the summer of 2008 designed to tighten regulation of the ailing Congressionally chartered mortgage giants Fannie Mae and Freddie Mac. Lenders that use the H4H program can refinance troubled borrowers into a new federally insured mortgage where the interest rate stays fixed for 30 years. The mortgage amount can be reduced to a maximum of 90 percent of the home's current appraised value, but there are equity sharing provisions where the homeowner must share some of the upside appreciation on the refinanced home with Uncle Sam.

HOPE NOW alliance   A business alliance of mortgage lenders, servicers, professional trade organizations, and credit counselors whose stated mission is to modify and restructure mortgages in an effort to help struggling home-owners avoid falling into foreclosure. The alliance says it uses two main tools: repayment plans where missed payments can be made up but the mortgage debt remains the same, and modifications where the original mortgage con-tract is permanently altered, including a reduction in the loan amount. The group claims it has helped more than two million homeowners prevent fore-closure since the summer of 2007 but has offered little in the way of hard evidence to bolster its claims. It has about 35 lender/servicer participants, including the nation's largest holders of mortgage contracts: Bank of America, Citigroup, JPMorgan Chase, and Wells Fargo. The group's phone number is: (888) 995-HOPE. Its web site: www.hopenow.com/.

jumbo mortgage   A loan whose dollar amount is above the Fannie Mae/ Freddie Mac loan limit, which was $417,000 up until early 2008. The ceiling was increased to just over $729,750 by mid-2008 to help lenders and home-owners living in areas of high-cost housing.

loan broker   A mortgage professional who offers different loan products to the consumer. The broker does not use his or her own money to originate the loan. The money comes from a wholesale lender (a firm like Wells Fargo, Countrywide, etc.). The broker receives a fee from the wholesale lender once the transaction closes. The wholesale lender funds and then owns the loan.

loan production or loan funding   A process that entails the origination of a mortgage to a consumer. The phrases loan production, loan funding, and loan origination are synonymous.

loan-to-value (LTV) ratio   When a mortgage is originated, the LTV is a calculation that shows how much cash or equity the home buyer is putting into the house. If a homeowner makes a $10,000 down payment on a $100,000 house and takes out a mortgage of $90,000, the LTV would be 90 percent.

loan trader   A professional who buys and sells (trades) loans for a living. The loans are sold to the trader by a mortgage lending company such as a bank, S&L, or nonbank lender. A loan trader might work at a Wall Street firm or a large lender like Wells Fargo.

mortgage-backed security (MBS) A bond backed (collateralized) by residential loans. The term MBS usually refers to A paper bonds that are guaranteed by Fannie Mae or Freddie Mac, but not always. MBSs can range in size from several hundred million dollars into the billions.

mortgage broker *See* loan broker.

mortgage insurance A policy issued by one of the nation's seven mortgage insurance firms that generally covers up to 20 percent of a lender's loss on a delinquent loan. (Not all types of loans are eligible for mortgage insurance.) The private mortgage insurance firms operating in the United States are the PMI Group, MGIC, Genworth Financial, Radian, United Guaranty, Republic Mortgage Insurance, and Triad (Triad is not writing new policies).

nonbank lender or nondepository A mortgage lender that finances its residential originations by borrowing money from a Wall Street firm or commercial bank. Nonbanks do not offer deposit accounts to the public and are not registered by a federal bank or S&L regulator.

Patriot Act Signed into law by President Bush on October 26, 2001, the act's official title is: Uniting and Strengthening America by Providing Appropriate Tools Required to Intercept and Obstruct Terrorism Act of 2001. The law gives law enforcement agencies additional tools to search the records of individuals and companies, including nonprofits. Areas where greater searches can be carried out include the monitoring of telephone calls, e-mails, medical and financial records—all without much judicial review.

payment option ARM (POA) An adjustable rate loan where the consumer is offered four different payment plans each month, including negative amortization where a low monthly payment (if this option is used) can actually increase the debt owed to the holder of the loan.

primary market A term used to describe the actual origination of a loan, where the loan process begins. After a loan is originated and funded, it might be sold in what is considered a secondary market transaction.

retail origination A mortgage made directly from a lending institution to a consumer with no intermediary (broker) being involved in the transaction.

A retail origination can be done through a branch, over the Internet, or though some other direct-to-consumer channel.

reverse auction   In regard to the $700 billion bailout program, the Treasury Department will buy pools of mortgages or bonds from sellers under TARP. In a reverse auction many different sellers might bring their assets—which are similar in nature (all subprime loans originated in 2006, for instance)—to the Treasury for sale. The Treasury will ask the sellers what the lowest price is they are willing to accept. The agency will then pick a winner of the auction, based on the lowest price.

secondary market   After a loan has been originated to a consumer (in the primary market) and then sold to another company, it is considered a secondary market transaction. Fannie Mae and Freddie Mac are two large secondary market companies that buy loans from mortgage banking firms. A loan, like a bond, can change hands more than once.

second lien or second mortgage   These are often home equity loans that are taken out after a first mortgage has already been recorded. On a new home purchase sometimes both a first and second mortgage (lien) are recorded at the same time, but the first always has priority (must be paid off first).

securitize   To issue a bond backed by a pool (group) of mortgages.

servicing   This entails the monthly processing of a loan, including collecting the payment from the consumer and passing on the principal, interest, taxes, and other charges to the proper parties. For doing this each month, the company (the servicer) receives a fee. Servicing is a separate business from lending, although the two businesses are related (for obvious reasons).

short sale   This involves the sale of a home where the lender allows the property to be sold for less than the amount owed on the mortgage and takes a loss. The seller of the home agrees to do this because he or she is having trouble making the mortgage payments. The lender that holds the mortgage approves a short sale because the price being offered might result in a smaller loss on the mortgage than if the house had gone into foreclosure.

stated-income or liar loan   A mortgage where the consumer states his or her income without the lender asking for documentation of the salary stated. The lender accepts the income stated "as is" because the borrower has a FICO score north of 700, which is considered A paper or prime quality.

subprime mortgage (loan)   A loan originated by a lender that is A− to D in quality. Consumers who have the best credit ratings with the highest FICO scores are considered A credit quality. Subprime borrowers usually have several blemishes on their credit histories, such as missed payments on mortgages and other types of installment debt including credit cards.

Treasury Department   A cabinet-level agency that manages the nation's revenue. The Treasury secretary is appointed by the president. In regard to the $700 billion bailout, the Treasury secretary—in this case Henry Paulson—has taken the lead in shaping legislation that gives his agency the power to buy troubled mortgages and other assets from hundreds of sellers. Paulson eventually approved a plan (which he was initially against) to use $125 billion of the TARP money to buy ownership stakes in nine of the nation's largest banks.

Troubled Asset Relief Program (TARP)   A government program legislated into existence in the fall of 2008 with the passage of the Emergency Economic Stabilization Act. Under TARP the Treasury Department agrees to buy mostly delinquent mortgage assets from banks, S&Ls, Wall Street firms, and other sellers. The program also allows the Treasury Department to buy ownership stakes in banks.

whole loan   A loan that represents the original residential mortgage before it has been securitized. Mortgages that have not been securitized are said to exist in whole loan form on the balance sheet of a bank, thrift, credit union, and so on. After many mortgages have been pooled into a security, the underlying whole loans often reside in a trust, a legal entity that is overseen by an administrator, often a bank or some other financial services firm.

wholesale lender   A mortgage company that uses loan brokers to find customers for them. A wholesaler does not employ loan brokers but pays the broker a fee once the mortgage actually closes. The wholesaler supplies a check at the closing table to fund the mortgage being made to the consumer.

About the Author

Paul Muolo is co-author of *Chain of Blame: How Wall Street Caused the Mortgage and Credit Crisis* (John Wiley & Sons, 2008) as well as *Inside Job: The Looting of America's Savings and Loans* (HarperCollins, 1991), a *New York Times* best seller. He also is executive editor of *National Mortgage News*, the leading independent trade publication/web site for the residential finance industry. Over the years his articles have appeared in *Barron's*, the *Sunday New York Times*, the *Washington Post*, *EuroMoney*, *Playboy*, and other publications. He has appeared as a guest on mortgage, real estate, and banking issues on ABC, CNN, CNBC, and Fox Business Network. *Inside Job* won several journalism awards, including the Investigative Reporters and Editors best book of the year and the Adult Editors Book Award. It was nominated for a Pulitzer Prize. He lives in Maryland with his wife and two daughters.